NEW NETHERLAND ROOTS

I0027227

Marriage Intention of Coenradt ten Eyck and Maria Boel in
the Dutch Reformed Church of Amsterdam, the Netherlands.

NEW
NETHERLAND
ROOTS

By

Gwenn F. Epperson

CLEARFIELD

Reprinted for
Clearfield Company by
Genealogical Publishing Co.
Baltimore, Maryland
2008

ISBN-13: 978-0-8063-1400-6
ISBN-10: 0-8063-1400-1

Made in the United States of America

Copyright © 1994
by Gwenn F. Epperson
All Rights Reserved
Published by Genealogical Publishing Co., Inc.
1001 N. Calvert St., Baltimore, MD. 21202
Second printing 1995
Library of Congress Catalogue Card Number 93-80320

The monogram on the cover of the book is taken from the seal of New Amsterdam which was designed in Holland and sent by the Company to Stuyvesant, who gave it to the Magistrates of the city on December 8, 1654 . . . . The monogram stands for the Geoctroyerde Westindische Compagnie (The Chartered West India Company).

DEDICATION

To the goodness and mercy of God whose guidance led our stalwart and enterprising ancestors across a raging sea to carve out of a wilderness the foundation for a great nation which is now known as America; and inspired the author to write this book.

CONTENTS

Contents

APPENDIXES

FOREWORD

When Peter Stuyvesant surrendered New Netherland to the English in 1664, the colony had less than 10,000 inhabitants, but today the descendants of those few colonists number in the millions. It is therefore not at all unusual for present-day genealogists to find that they have one or more ancestral lines that go back to that remote Dutch settlement. In the extensive records of New Netherland, and its successors New York and New Jersey, the researcher discovers a richly diverse society, notably different from those of its neighbors. More often than not, the records name the place where a European settler lived before coming to the New World. The curious researcher will naturally want to follow this lead, in the hope of finding more ancestry on the other side of the Atlantic.

Over the past seven years, Gwenn F. Epperson has written a series of articles tracing early settlers of New Netherland back to their roots in the Netherlands, Germany, Belgium and France. That these articles were published in one of the most highly regarded scholarly genealogical journals, *The New York Genealogical and Biographical Record*, attests to the quality of Mrs. Epperson's work. What sets her articles apart from others on the same subject is the fact that she did all of the research herself, despite the fact that she is not a professional genealogist and has only limited knowledge of languages other than English--and, even more important, that she did all her research not in Europe, but in the Family History Library at Salt Lake City, in her home state of Utah.

Over the past few decades the Family History Library has collected, on microfilm and microfiche, copies of original records from many countries, and made them available to researchers not only in Salt Lake City but at Family History Centers worldwide. Included in the collection are thousands of films from the Netherlands and other countries that produced settlers of New Netherland. Yet few genealogists descended from these settlers seem to have tried to make use of these resources, either because they have not known that they were available, or because they assumed that they would be too difficult to use. Most research on the settlers' ancestry continues to be done, as in the past, by European researchers hired by those few descendants who can afford the fees.

Noting Mrs. Epperson's success, I suggested that she try to write an article explaining, step by step, how to use the Family History Library for this type of research. It soon became clear that the subject would be more appropriately presented in a small book. This guide is the result.

Before research in European records can begin, it is almost essential that the settler's European place of origin be known. If it has not been found, Mrs. Epperson lists numerous New Netherland sources where that vital piece of information might still be awaiting discovery. The researcher will, in any case, want to be sure that all of these New Netherland sources have been utilized before turning to the European indexes, gazetteers, maps, church records and other resources which are also carefully described.

Mrs. Epperson has selected publications and microfilm sources that she feels can be handled even by the researcher who knows no language other than English. She makes it clear, however, that the researcher is going to encounter records written in outmoded forms of unfamiliar languages, often in a handwriting that differs markedly from that in use today. Obviously some will be able to go further with these resources than will others, and in the end everyone may reach a point where further European research, if necessary, can only be done in Europe or by someone very much at home with the language and handwriting. If that point is reached, the genealogist who has already become somewhat familiar with the European records by using this book will be in a much better position to work intelligently with a European researcher than one who has made no attempt in that direction.

For some New Netherland families, of course, research across the Atlantic has already been done, sometimes many years ago. This book can still be relevant in such cases, as the careful genealogist will always try to re-check earlier findings, even those long in print and widely accepted. It may turn out that the earlier researcher missed or misinterpreted a crucial document, and the claimed ancestry must be totally reconsidered. While pioneer work on the origins of New Netherland families was sometimes done by true experts, such as the late William J. Hoffman, F.A.S.G., there were also those whose writings must always be viewed with suspicion. The late Louis P. de Boer, for example, concocted fraudulent ancestries for a number of the early Dutch colonists.

Every genealogist who is descended from a New Netherland family should study this guide. Hopefully Mrs. Epperson's suggestions will help them discover the names of long-lost European forbears and add to our knowledge of those brave colonists who crossed the Atlantic to New Netherland over three centuries ago.

Harry Macy, Jr., F.A.S.G.

PREFACE

For years I was assured by professional researchers that foreign genealogical research in ancient records could only be accomplished by a native of the country.

I refused to accept this position, remembering the pride exhibited by family members when old Coenradt ten Eyck, their immigrant ancestor from "Holland," was mentioned. This link with the past was important, because it helped the family to establish their identity. How wonderful it would be to find and visit Coenradt ten Eyck's place of origin for a nostalgic reunion!

In 1980 I had the pleasure of visiting Coenradt's birthplace in Moers, *Germany*, not Holland, but close to the Dutch border. By chance Hendrik O. Slok, a Dutch genealogist in Salt Lake City (now deceased), located the marriage intention of Coenradt ten Eyck in the indexes to the church records of Amsterdam and offered me the information for the price of repairs on his car. With the place of origin found in this record I was able to locate Coenradt ten Eyck's baptism in the Reformed Church of Moers.

This incident points up the fact that, when the client cannot afford to pay a native-born genealogist to research a country's very old records, it is the task of family members with genuine feelings for their ancestors to do the work, and invariably the ways and means will be provided. Almost all researchers can tell the story of a miraculous find after they had appeared to reach a dead end.

The purpose of this guidebook is to demonstrate that the reader can also trace a seventeenth-century New Netherland ancestor back to the place of origin in Europe using a few simple techniques described in the book.

I would like to pay special tribute to a dedicated editor, Harry Macy, Jr., F.A.S.G., who has been a good friend and mentor over the years. Without his expertise the book could not have been written.

Of course, the excellent facilities for genealogical research and record preservation provided by the Family History Library of The Church of Jesus Christ of Latter-day Saints in Salt Lake City, and their family history centers located in many countries are world renowned. Through their services it is often easier to do foreign research in Salt Lake City than abroad. Most of the research for this book was accomplished in this great facility, with the expert advice of their research consultants.

Another organization due honorable mention is the New York Genealogical and Biographical Society, with its wonderful staff and library. I wish to thank the Society for granting me permission to include in this book several of my articles originally published in the *Record*, as well as one by Hendrick O. Slock.

I extend my warmest thanks to Dr. Arlene H. Eakle of Woods Cross, Utah, who is co-author with Vincent L. Jones and Mildred Christensen of the excellent textbook *Genealogical Research: A Jurisdictional Approach* (Salt Lake City Utah: Publishers Press, 1972) and was my instructor. Without her efficient note-keeping system, I could not possibly have undertaken this book, using material gathered over a twenty-year period.

Credit also goes to Hendrik (Hank) O. Slok, already mentioned, who tutored me in the intricacies of Dutch research and is the author of the excellent research papers on genealogical sources in the Netherlands, published by the Family History Library.

My greatest appreciation goes to my husband, Larry Epperson, who typed the manuscript, and my grandson, David L. Nuttall, who put the manuscript into camera-ready form for publication.

INTRODUCTION

Those with seventeenth-century "New Netherland" ancestors are fortunate indeed! These forbears often left distinct "footprints in the sands of time" by supplying their all-important place of origin in the so-called passenger lists of the Dutch West India Company, early Dutch Church marriage registers, and other records of New Netherland. In this guide, each of these sources will be discussed, as will exact steps to follow, and research aids to use, in establishing these families in Europe. The text includes many examples from research by the author and others. (It will, of course, be the responsibility of the reader to first research the family in America back to the immigrant ancestor before attempting research in Europe.)

The popular image of the people who came out with the Dutch West India Company is that most of them were "Dutch," but research in both European and American records proves many were refugees to the Netherlands from what is now Belgium, Germany, France, Scandinavia, and Great Britain. Therefore, the researcher may lose a "Dutch" ancestor or two in the research process, but gain a more varied ancestry.

ILLUSTRATIONS

Illustration 1: Citizenship Record of Coenradt ten Eyck in Amsterdam, the Netherlands.

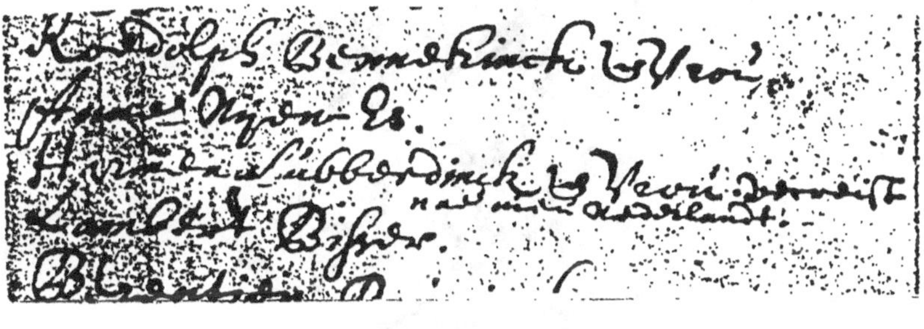

Illustration 2: Membership Record of Harmen Lubberdinck and his wife in the Dutch Reformed Church of Geesteren, the Netherlands.

Illustration 3: Baptism of Aloff, son of Peter vom Remscheidt, and Gierdt, daughter of Lucas Barss, in the Reformed Church of Elberfeld, Germany.

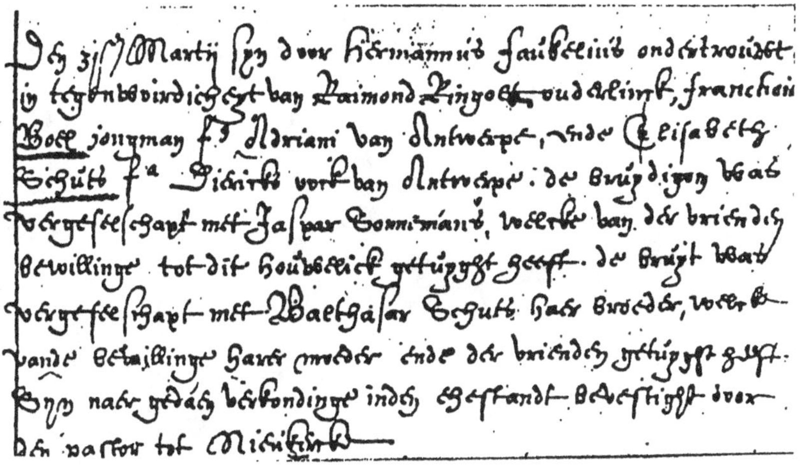

Illustration 4: Marriage Intention of Franchois Boel, son of Adrian from Antwerp, and Elisabeth Schuts, daughter of Dierick also from Antwerp, in the Dutch Reformed Church of Cologne, Germany.

Illustration 5: Baptism of Frans Boel, son of Adrian Boel and Cornelia, in the Onze Lieve Vrow Roman Catholic Church of Antwerp, Belgium.

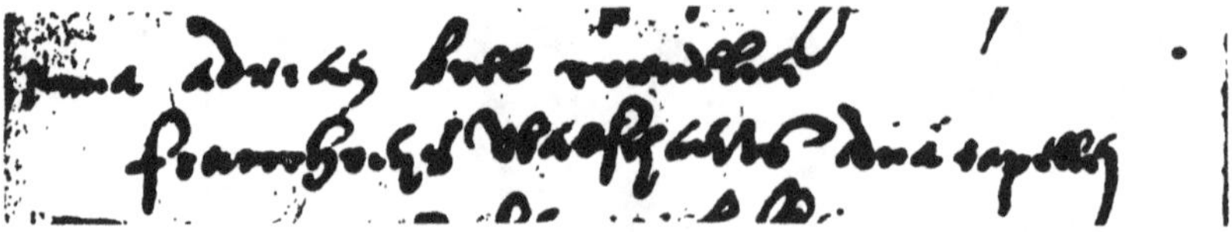

Illustration 6: Baptism of Anna, daughter of Adrian Boel and Cornelia, in the Onze Lieve Vrow Roman Catholic Church of Antwerp, Belgium.

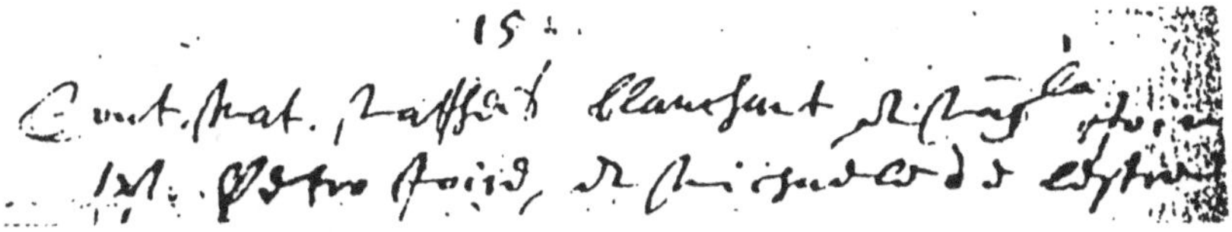

Illustration 7: Marriage of Matthew Blanchan and Magdalena Joire in the Roman Catholic Church of Armentières, France.

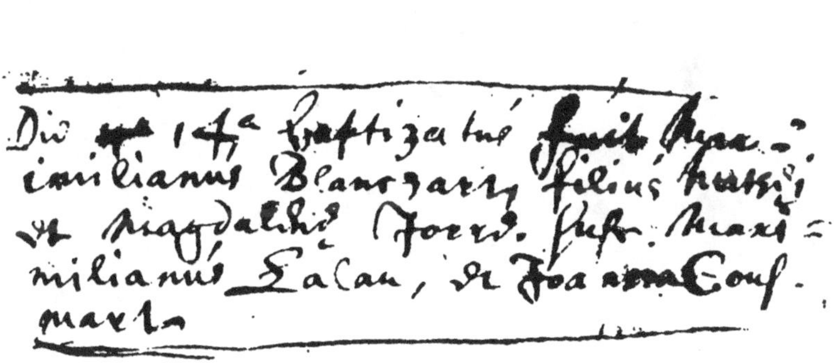

Illustration 8: Baptism of Maximilianus, son of Matthew Blanchan and Magdalena Joire, in the Roman Catholic Church of Armentières, France.

NEW NETHERLAND ROOTS

1   ESTABLISHING THE PLACE OF ORIGIN IN NEW NETHERLAND RECORDS

"Passenger Lists"

The West India Company Account Book

One of the most important sources of information concerning the origin of immigrants to New Netherland during the Dutch period is an old account book of the Dutch West India Company listing passengers coming on credit.[1] The left side of the ledger lists the charges for bringing over the parties named, and the right side the payments for same.

As the published versions of the records have not always been accurate, astute researchers prefer to consult the original account book. Fortunately, a microfilm copy is now available at the library of the New York Genealogical and Biographical Society, the New York Public Library, and the New York State Library.

Since the original account book is in seventeenth-century Dutch, and the scribbled entries on the credit side of the ledger are almost illegible, most researchers rely on several translations in print, the best of which is by Arnold J.F. van Laer, a Dutchman and former New York State Archivist.[2] A less complete version is given in Edmund B. O'Callaghan's *Documentary History of the State of New York* and reprinted

---

[1] New York Colonial Manuscripts, vol. 14, pp. 83-123, formerly Book KK, Accounts 1654-1664, pp. 1-90, original in New York State Archives.

[2] Arnold J.F. van Laer, trans., "Passengers to New Netherland: List of Passengers, 1654-1664," from *New York Colonial Mss.*, vol. 14, pp. 83-123, in *Year Book of the Holland Society of New York*, hereafter HSYB (1902): 1-37; Family History Library microfilm, hereafter FHL 0908989, item [it.] 5.

in *Lists of Inhabitants of Colonial New York.*[3]

These translations are presented in the format of passenger lists giving the dates of sailing, names of ships in Dutch and English, names of skippers and passengers. As in the originals, in some cases the wives, the children (including their ages), and other relatives or servants are mentioned but usually not named. Occasionally the person's trade is added, as is most importantly the place of origin, although often misspelled and difficult to locate on any current map. Indexes both by names and places are also included. However, no entries from the credit side of the ledger are given.

For the greatest accuracy these translations should be used in conjunction with the original account book on microfilm and an article by Rosalie Fellows Bailey "Emigrants to New Netherland: Account Book 1654-1664."[4] Bailey obtained her information from James Riker's notes on the account book.[5] When compared to the previously mentioned translations, Riker's notes reveal "new names, new marriages, and relationships, new occupations, or employers, new residences and deaths."[6] A good understanding of the account book may be obtained by reading Bailey's article, which includes translations of some of the credit entries. It must be added, however, as stated by Bailey:

---

[3] Edmund B. O'Callaghan, ed., *The Documentary History of the State of New York*, 4 vols. in 8 (Albany: Weed, Parson & Co., public printers, 1849). vol. 3, pt. 1, 52-63; FHL 0896505, it. 2, MF 6051121.

[4] Rosalie Fellows Bailey, "Emigrants to New Netherland: Account Book 1654-1664," *New York Genealogical and Biographical Record*, hereafter the *Record* and REC. 94 (1963): 193-200.

[5] "List of Emigrants to New Netherland, 1654-1664," MS. pamphlet in Box 23, James Riker Collection, Rare Books and Manuscripts Division, New York Public Library.

[6] Bailey, "Emigrants," p. 193.

They *are not full lists* of the passengers which came out in said vessels on the respective date. . . . Passengers on paid "tickets" naturally are not listed in the account book-- unless they owe for others. . . . Many more credit entries remain untranslated.[7]

The following are examples from the author's research illustrating the use of these passenger lists to obtain the places of origin, occupations, and relationships of early immigrants to New Netherland. The first gives only the place of origin:

17 May 1658. In *De Vergulde Bever (The Gilded Beaver)*, Captain Jan Reyersz Van der Beets.

Jan Evertsen, from Lookeren.[8]

However, the wife of Jan Evertsen came over also. Her entry gives much additional information and locks in their identification, thus forming the basis for research in European records for the article "Jan Evertsen, Master Shoemaker of Albany" which is scheduled for future publication:

8 April 1662. In *De Hoop (The Hope)*, Captain Pieter Emilius.

Annetie Hendricx, wife of Jan Evertsen, shoemaker in New Netherland, and five children, 14, 12, 9, 7, and 6 years old.[9]

"Lookeren" can be identified as Lokeren, Oost Vlaanderen (East Flanders), Belgium, formerly part of the Spanish Netherlands. Unfortunately Lockeren could not be established as Jan Evertsen's place of origin from its extant Catholic church registers. Although the parish registers of Lokeren's St. Lambertus start in 1586, his baptism was not

---

[7] Ibid., pp. 193, 198.

[8] HSYB (1902): 7; FHL 0908989, it. 5.

[9] Ibid., p. 20.

found.

The next illustration gives the origin as only a general area, too difficult to research, especially when the immigrant used a patronymic rather than a fixed surname:

> 12 February 1659. In *De Trouw (The Faith)*, Captain Jan Jansen Bestevaer.
>
> Pieter Cornelisz, laborer, from Holstein.[10]

This man was known as Pieter Cornelisz Low. Holstein apparently refers to the area which forms half of the German state of Schleswig-Holstein. For a complete workup on this Low family, using the passenger lists among other records, the reader is referred to the author's article "Another Low Family of New York and New Jersey."[11]

An entry for a Huguenot ancestor, Matthew Blanchan, is also found in these records. It gives his occupation, place of origin, a wife, and the ages of his three children. Just below, his daughter and her husband, Anthony Crispel, are listed as coming on the same ship:

> 26 April 1660. In *De Vergulde Otter (The Gilded Otter)*, Captain Cornelis Reyersz Van der Beets.
>
> Mattheus Blanchand, farmer, from Artois, wife and three children, 12, 9, and 5 years old.
> Anthony Krypel, farmer, from Artois, and wife.[12]

Artois was at this time a province in the northern tip of France, now a part of the Departement Pas de Calais. An exact place of origin for the Blanchan family was given in

---

[10] Ibid., p. 8.

[11] Gwenn F. Epperson, "Another Low Family of New York and New Jersey," REC. 119 (1988): 193-201; 120 (1989): 35-43, 104-07.

[12] HSYB (1902): 16; FHL 0908989, it. 5.

other records which will be discussed later. An entry for another man the author has researched gives a wife and the age of a son coming with the couple but no place of origin. However, their son-in-law is mentioned, which further establishes the identity of their daughter:

> 23 December 1660. In *De Trouw (The Faith)*, Captain Jan Jansz Bestevaer.
>
> Adolf Hardenbroeck, wife and son, 25 years old. (Pieter Rudolphus agrees to pay passage for the son of Adolph Hardenbroeck).[13]

Four years later another son of Adolph is found on the passenger lists, this time giving the all-important place of origin, a wife, and the ages of four children accompanying them. This information, coupled with early Dutch Church marriage records, to be discussed later, started the author on research in Europe which resulted in an article on this family.[14]

> 20 January 1664. In *De Trouw (The Faith)*, Captain Jan Jansz Bestevaer.
>
> Johannis Hardenbroeck, from Elbervelt [Elberfeld], wife and four children, 8, 6, 5 and three years old.[15]

Van Rensselaer Papers

Another list of immigrants to New Netherland worth researching contains the place of origin for approximately

---

[13] Ibid.

[14] Gwenn F. Epperson, "The European Origin of the Hardenbrook Family," REC. 117 (1986): 1-7; reprinted as Appendix B in this guide.

[15] HSYB (1902): 27; FHL 0908989, it. 5.

one-third of the persons mentioned. These immigrants were brought over by the patroon Kiliaen Van Rensselaer to work on his manor Rensselaerswyck, in the Hudson River Valley around the present city of Albany. The list is entitled "Settlers in Rensselaerswyck from 1630 to 1646," compiled from Van Rensselaer's "Books of Monthly Wages and Other Manuscripts,"[16] and first published in O'Callaghan's *History of New Netherland*.[17] The Van Rensselaer list also appears at the end of an article by the late Dutch-American genealogist William J. Hoffman,[18] reprinted by Carl Boyer, 3rd, in his book on passengers to the middle colonies.[19]

A more complete list of Rensselaerswyck settlers is found in the *Van Rensselaer Bowier Manuscripts*, edited by Van Laer.[20] While the list at the back of this book probably gives all the places of origin found in the text, the latter should always be checked as well for additional details. In the introduction to the book Van Laer explains the flaws in several earlier publications of this list and his reason for republication, as well as outlining the contents:

In view of the incompleteness of the list of settlers of the

---

[16] E.B. O'Callaghan, comp., "Settlers in Rensselaerswyck from 1630 to 1646." Comp. from Van Rensselaer's "Books of Monthly Wages and Other Manuscripts," HSYB (1896): 130-40; FHL 0908989, it. 1.

[17] E. B. O'Callaghan, *History of New Netherland*, 2 vols. (New York: D. Appleton & Co., 1846-48), 1: 429-44; not microfilmed, hereafter n.m.

[18] William J. Hoffman, "Random Notes Concerning Settlers of Dutch Descent," *The American Genealogist*, hereafter TAG 29 (April 1953): 65-76, 146-52; 30 (January 1954): 138-44; FHL 1320924, its. 9 & 10.

[19] Carl Boyer, 3rd, *Ship Passenger Lists, New York and New Jersey, 1600-1825* (Newhall, Calif.: the compiler, 1978); FHL microfiche, hereafter MF 6048671.

[20] Arnold J.F. van Laer, trans. and ed., *Van Rensselaer Bowier Manuscripts* (Albany: University of the State of New York, 1908), pp. 805-46; n.m.

colony of Rensselaerswyck furnished by Mr. de Roever [late archivist of the City of Amsterdam], who had access to the Van Rensselaer Bowier manuscripts only, and the many errors in the similar list published by O'Callaghan, whose researchers were confined to the Rensselaerswyck manuscripts, it has seemed worthwhile to prepare from the two sources named an entirely new list, which should adequately illustrate the growth of the colony and furnish a reliable means of identification of the persons mentioned in the present papers.

This list will be found at the end of the volume. It covers the period of settlement up to 1658, when the papers in the volume strictly relating to Rensselaerswyck cease. The list gives in brief form as far as they could be ascertained the principal data as to name, date of arrival, occupation and place of origin of each individual settler and throws much new light on the large proportion of elements other than Dutch that entered into the population of the colony.[21]

Some of the names from this list are included:

1630

By de Eendracht

Sailed from the Texel, 21 March 1630; arrived at New Amsterdam, 24 May 1630.

Claes Claesz, from Vlecker [Fleckero, an island off the south coast of Norway] . . . .

Wolfert Gerritsz, from Amersfoort; occasionally referred to as Wolfert Gerritsz van Conwenhoven, Conwenhoven, being a farm or estate about four miles northwest of Amersfoort, in the province of Utrecht.

Pieter Hendricksz from Soest, [presumably the village of that name in the province of Utrecht, but possibly the city of Soest in Westphalia]; . . . .

---

[21] Ibid., pp. 32-33.

Roelof Jansz, from Masterland [Marstrand, on the coast of Sweden]; . . . .

Seger (Zeeger) Jansz, from Nykerk, [province of Gelderland]; . . . .[22]

Amsterdam Notarial Abstracts

An additional source of information for passengers to New Netherland was very kindly brought to the author's attention by the Associate Editor of the *Record*, Harry Macy, Jr., F.A.S.G., who states:

> Previous mention has been made in the *Record* (113:193; 116:244; 120:138) of the collection of 5,000 abstracts pertaining to North America, mostly taken from Amsterdam notarial records and housed in a card index at the Amsterdam Municipal Archives as well as on film at the New York State Library (microfilm A-FM 200-1). Entitled 'Noord Amerika Chronologie,' the abstracts cover the years 1598-1750 and contain many items that have still not been recognized for their genealogical value.[23]

Then Mr. Macy quotes from Hoffman's article "Random Notes Concerning Settlers of Dutch Descent":

> During the many years that de Roever was in charge of the Amsterdam archives, he collected every bit of information relating to the Dutch settlers, taken principally from notarial papers. The notes were all written in very small but legible handwriting on little bits of paper only partly filed in alphabetical order and therefore difficult to consult. The greater part of this collection was later acquired by the Koninklyk Nederlandsch Genootschap

---

[22] Ibid., pp. 805-06.

[23] Harry Macy, Jr., "Jochem Kaller/Caljer/Colyer: His Place of Origin Identified," REC. 121 (1990): 36.

voor Geslacht en Wapenkunde at The Hague. . . .[24]

Hoffman goes on to say:

> The collection proved to be somewhat of a disappointment in
> some respects, as many of the data had already been used by de
> Roever and in the "V.R.B. [Van Rensselaer Bowier] Papers" and
> it contained very little or no information about some of the
> important, still unsolved genealogical problems . . . . Nevertheless,
> it did disclose many facts of interest.
>
> Taken in large measure from depositions made before various
> Notaries Public at Amsterdam (the majority being powers-of-
> attorney to hire servants or to collect money either in New
> Netherland or Patria),[25] the facts stated therein--in most cases
> made under oath--are authentic and in addition were taken down
> by persons who were expert in noting such details as places of
> origin, age, correct names, and relationships.[26]

Some of the notarial abstracts contain information on
people departing for New Netherland and therefore serve as
a form of "passenger list." Most of the abstracts are not
directly related to migration, but they do give places of
origin.

An example of these records given by Hoffman and
relevant to the author's research is as follows:

> Coenraet ten Eyck, master shoemaker and tanner at New
> Amsterdam, engaged Abel Hardenbroeck from Elberfeld,
> Germany [see *NY Rec*, 1939: 130] on 6 Jan. 1659 [Not. H. Schaeff]
> to serve him in his shoeshop, his tannery, and at "the vats."[27]

---

[24] William J. Hoffman, "Random Notes Concerning Settlers of Dutch
Descent," TAG 29 (April 1953): 65; FHL 1320924, it. 9.

[25] Patria: Latin for "Fatherland." Was used in New Netherland to refer
to the Netherlands.

[26] TAG 29: 66.

[27] Ibid., pp. 69-70.

Another reference to an ancestor, Symon Volckerts
Veeder, is even more detailed and also mentions the place
of origin:

> Hendrik Willems, the leading baker at New Amsterdam in
> the second half of the 17th century [Icon. Manh. II:261] was a
> native of the small town of Esens in Holstein as specified in a
> mention of him as a "baker in New Netherland" [2 Feb. 1650, Not.
> H. van Velsen], when *Joost Theunissen* from Norden, also a baker
> at New Amsterdam, but in Amsterdam at the time, hired for
> Hendrik the baker's apprentice *Symon Volckerts* from Esens,
> Holstein.[28]

The following abstract further confirms the former
residence of the Van Borsum family in Amsterdam, which
will be detailed later:

> A brother of *Egbert Van Borsum* was "spiegelkastenmaker"
> (showcase maker) at Amsterdam [25 Apr. 1659, Not. J. Hellerus,
> p. 204].[29]

Early Dutch Church Marriage Registers and Other Church Records

Other important sources used to establish the place of
origin for early New Netherland settlers are the marriage
registers of the earliest Dutch Churches,[30] i.e. New Amster-

---

[28] Ibid., p. 149.

[29] Ibid., pp. 150-51.

[30] Dutch Church: According to Russell L. Gasero, Archivist, Historical
Society of the Reformed Church in America, "During the colonial period,
the churches were addressed as the 'Reformed Dutch Churches in New
York and New Jersey.' In 1789, the title of the church was changed to
'Reformed Protestant Dutch Church.' Since 1867 the name has been 'The

dam (New York), Kingston, Brooklyn, Bergen, and Flatbush. Other Dutch Church marriage registers mostly begin after the immigrant generations had already married and references to European place names are sparse. Perhaps a short discussion concerning the state of religion during the Dutch rule of New Netherland will help explain the importance of the Dutch Church records. John P. Dern, in his introduction to *The Albany Protocol* says, "Since 1624 the [Dutch West India] Company had decreed the Reformed religion should be the only religion practiced publicly."[31]

The earliest official mention found by the author is contained in O'Callaghan's *Documents Relative to the Colonial History of the State of New York* taken from "Proposed Freedoms and Exemptions for New Netherland 1640: . . . granted and accorded by the Directors of the General Incorporated West India Company . . . to all Patroons, Masters, or Private persons who will plant any Colonies or introduce cattle in New Netherland. Exhibited 19th July 1640."[32] This document goes on to say:

> And no other Religion shall be publicly admitted in New Netherland except the Reformed, as it is at present preached and practiced by public authority in the United Netherlands; and for this purpose the Company shall provide and maintain good and suitable preachers, schoolmasters and comforters of the sick.[33]

Reformed Church in America." In a telephone conversation Gasero suggested using the accepted short form "Dutch Reformed Church," hereafter DRC.

[31] John Philip Dern, ed., *The Albany Protocol* (Ann Arbor, Michigan: Dern, 1971), p. xii; FHL 0930247, it. 4.

[32] E.B. O'Callaghan and Berthold Fernow, trans. and eds., *Documents Relative to the Colonial History of the State of New York*, 15 vols. (Albany: Weed, Parson & Co., 1856-1887), 1: 123. Reprint. Camden, Maine: Picton Press, 1992; FHL 0824380, it. 1.

[33] Ibid.

This situation prevailed until the British takeover of the colony in 1664 and freedom of religion was gradually established. However, few extant registers of other denominations predate the turn of the eighteenth century, and they rarely give any places of origin.

The New York City Dutch Church is the oldest of that denomination in America, and almost all marriage entries, which begin in 1639, contain the place of origin of both bride and groom. However, in many cases the spelling is badly distorted.[34]

The author is related to the first couple in the book. The marriage entry supplies the first evidence concerning the origin of these people, as they came over too early to be included in the surviving Dutch West India Company passenger lists. Their marriage entry reads as translated:

> 11 December [1639]. Egbert Van Borsum, young man from Embden [Emden], and Annetje Hendricks, young woman from Amsterdam.[35]

With the information found in this marriage record, and civil records described later in the text, the author was able to trace the Van Borsum and Hendricks families back to their European origins. The reader is directed to the author's article "The European Ancestry of Egbert Van Borsum and Annetje Hendricks" for further study.[36]

The marriage as translated of "Wessel Wesselszen, young man from Wessen [Wessum in the diocese Munster] and

---

[34] Samuel S. Purple, ed., *Marriages from 1639 to 1801 in the Reformed Dutch Church of New Amsterdam and New York City*. Collections of the New York Genealogical and Biographical Society, vol. 1 (New York: The Society, 1890. Reprint. vol. 9, 1940), hereafter MDC; FHL 0928042, it. 1, MF 6016531-4.

[35] MDC 10.

[36] Gwenn F. Epperson, "The European Ancestry of Egbert Van Borsum and Annetje Hendricks," REC. 119 (1988): 85-89.

Marritje ten Eyck, young woman from Amsterdam," on 17 December 1670,[37] also provided further evidence to support research for the author's article "The Ten Eyck-Boel European Connection."[68] Marritje was baptized in Amsterdam 2 April 1646, daughter of Coenradt Ten Eyck and Maria Boel.[39]

Three marriages in the New York Dutch Church were helpful in writing the Hardenbrook article, aforementioned.[40] The first as translated is that of the daughter of the immigrant ancestors Adolph Hardenbrook and Maria Caterberg:

10 October 1659. Pieter Rodolphus de Vries, widower of Francina Berck and Margariet Hardenbroeck from Ervervelt [Elberfeld].[41]

Another marriage record for a child of the Hardenbrooks is also found in the New York Dutch Church:

12 Nov. 1684. Hendrick Arentszen, young man from Zutphen, and Catharina Hardenbroeck, young daughter from Elbervelt, both living here.[42]

And the marriage of their nephew in the same church:

16 June 1686. Johannes Hardenbroeck, young man from Amsterdam, and Sara Van Laer, young woman from New York,

---

[37] MDC 34.

[38] Gwenn F. Epperson, "The Ten Eyck-Boel European Connection," REC. 118 (1987): 14-18, reprinted as Appendix C in this guide.

[39] Baptisms Oudekerk of Amsterdam, 8: n.p.; FHL 0113133.

[40] REC. 117 (1986): 1-7.

[41] MDC 24.

[42] Ibid., p. 55.

both living here.[43]

The next Dutch Church marriage registers useful for finding the European origins of early New Netherland settlers are those of Kingston, Ulster County, New York, which begin in 1660. In the preface to the published version the editor has this to say regarding these records:

> With this book commences the oldest original set now extant, of the Baptismal and Marriage Registers in the Dutch Church of this country. Those of the New York Church, previous to the settlement of Domine Henricus Selyns as its regular minister in 1682, are merely copies made by him from the records or memoranda of his predecessors, which, unhappily, are now lost or destroyed, while those of the Albany Church, previous to the pastorate of Domine Godefridus Dellius, which began in 1683, are no longer in existence. . . .
>
> The genealogical and historical value of the Kingston Church Registers cannot well be overestimated. They embrace the names of many Dutchmen who came directly from Holland two centuries and a half ago, some of whom made their first homes either in New York or Albany, and it may also be said that a very large portion of the Dutch families who immigrated to this country before the close of the 17th century are represented, to a greater or less extent, on these pages . . . . Nor do these records represent only the early family history of the Dutch. The names of the old Huguenot residents of Kingston and other places, many of whom subsequently removed to New Paltz, and of a large number of the Germans who settled at Newburgh and in Ulster, Dutchess, and Albany Counties in the early part of the last century [18th], as well as of numerous English families and a few Scotch and Irish, are here recorded, and information concerning them given that can be obtained from no other source.[44]

Examples from these marriage registers clearly demon-

---

[43] Ibid., p. 60.

[44] Roswell Randall Hoes, ed., *Baptismal and Marriage Registers of the Old Dutch Church of Kingston, Ulster County, New York, 1660-1809* (Baltimore: Genealogical Publishing Co., 1980); FHL 1294820, it. 4.

strate their value:

Item 21. 1667 [date of marriage not given] Jan Matthysen, j.m. of Fort Orangie, [Ft. Orange, now Albany], and Madalena Blanchan, j.d. of Engelant [England]. Banns published three times "in succession," 28 Sept. Married by the Hon. Justice.

Item 28. 1668 [date of marriage not given] Pieter Cornelissen [Low], and Elisabet Blansjan, j.d. Date of Banns not given.

Item 38. 30 Mar. 1679 Matys Blanjan, De Jonge [i.e., junior], j.m. of Manheim, in the Palts [Palatinate, now Mannheim, Baden-Württemburg, Germany], and Margarietje Claas Van Schoonhoove, j.d., from Nieu Albanien [New Albany]. In the absence of Domine Van Gaasbeeck, they were married in the church by the Secretary [of the village]. First publication of Banns, 1 March.

Although the marriage record of Elisabeth Blanchan does not give her place of origin, nevertheless the entry is included to demonstrate how records of siblings, i.e. Magdalena and Matthew in this case, may include the missing information. These marriage records indicate the Blanchan family resided in several places on their way to America, supplying additional areas for research.

Another church with early extant marriage records is the Brooklyn Dutch Church, as found in *Old First Dutch Reformed Church of Brooklyn, New York; First Book of Records 1660-1752*.[45] The introduction to these records states:

> The Marriage Register covers eight leaves in the Breuckelen Church Records, three of which are heavily damaged at the bottom, leaving a number of entries incomplete. ... Domine Henricus Selijns wrote the entries through July 1664. Hendrick Slecht listed all other marriages except the one on 26 January 1695. ... In spite of Slecht's longevity as a registrar, the list

---

[45] A.P.G. Jos van der Linde, trans. and ed., *New York Historical Manuscripts: Dutch, Old First Dutch Reformed Church of Brooklyn, New York: First Book of Records, 1660-1752* (Baltimore: Genealogical Publishing Co., 1983); n.m. (Another version of these records in the 1897 *Year Book of the Holland Society of New York* is unreliable and should not be used.)

shows considerable gaps throughout the three decades following Selijns' departure in 1664.[46]

Fortunately the book includes in Appendix B an "Explanatory List of Geographic Names Mentioned in the Breuckelen Church Records." The editor says:

> In the Registers of Baptisms, Marriages, and Members of the Congregation, however, the original spelling of the geographic names has been reproduced between quotation marks. Many of the geographical terms applied in 17th- and 18th-century Dutch manuscripts are now obsolete or hard to recognize because of a distorted spelling. For this reason, all geographical names mentioned in the Breuckelen Church Records were included in an explanatory list appended to this book.[47]

An example of these marriage records is included:

1662, July 25:
- by Domine Megapolensis:
Henricus Selijns, "from Amsterd[am]" to Mechtelina Specht, "from Uijtrecht" with certificate "from Uytrecht," and after three proclamations of banns "in N[ieuw] Amsterd[am] and Breuckelen."[48]

While the marriage registers of the Brooklyn Dutch Church contain the most references to the origins of its members, the membership lists cannot be overlooked. They reveal some additional places of origin not included in the marriage registers.

Marriages of the Dutch Church of Bergen, New Jersey begin in 1665. Although at first glance they appear not to contain places of origin, this changes in 1672 and approximately half of the marriages then give the names of European places. Also, many include province names for better

---

[46] Ibid., pp. xxvi-xxvii.

[47] Ibid., p. xxix.

[48] Ibid., p. 212.

identification.[49] From 1668 to 1676 all the marriages except one were performed either by the court at Bergen or by the minister in New York, indicating the church was not supplied by a qualified minister at that time. Of the quality and preparation of the work, a statement is taken from the introduction to the published records:

> All names have been faithfully copied as they appear with all the variations in spellings and errors of the voorlesers; and where omissions occur, even though possible to supply, no inserts have been made. The record is thought to be truly represented. All entries have been arranged in the order of their dates . . . and consecutively numbered for convenience in indexing.

The countries represented vary greatly and include the Netherlands, Scotland, Barbados, England, Germany, and France (one even "born at sea"). Several examples of the Bergen Dutch Church marriage records are included to demonstrate the rich variety of nationalities:

17 July 28, 1672. Lourus Arense Toers, Y.M., from Amsterdam, Holland, and Francyntje Tomas, Y.D., from New York, married at New York 15 Aug. 1672.

33 March 11, 1678. Charles Macheleen, Y.M., from Scotland, and Catryna Thomas, Y.D., from Barbadoes. Received certificate 26 March 1678.

34 May 26, 1678. Joseph Arsele, Y.M., from London, O. England, and Elisabeth Walinghs, Y.D., from Wickham in O. England.

67 November 2, 1684. Isaac Billau, Y.M., born at sea, and Ida Sueberingh, Y.D., from Midwout, L.I. Received certificate to Staten Is. 25 Nov.

---

[49] Dingman Versteeg and Thomas E. Vermilye, Jr., trans. and eds., *Bergen Records, Records of the Reformed Protestant Dutch Church of Bergen in New Jersey, 1666 to 1788*, 3 bks. in 1 (Baltimore: Genealogical Publishing Co., 1976) 2: 57-65; reprinted from HSYB (1914): 57-85; FHL 1405485, it. 11.

81 September 20, 1687. Pieter Pierra, Y.M., from Sedan, France,
living at Hackensack, and Weyntje Cornelis (widow of Poulis
Jansen) living at Bergen, had certificate, that they had been
registered by the French Preacher at New York, to have their first
bans [sic] published on 25 September. After the publication of
bans [sic] on three Sundays . . . they were married 19 October by
R. Van Giesen in presence of the Bergen court.

85 May 13, 1688. Andries Preyer, Y.M. from Crevelt in County
Meurs [Germany] and Johanna Steynmetz, Y.D., from Bergen,
both living at Ahasymus. Were Married after three proclamations
of bans [sic].

Although Flatbush was among the earliest Dutch Churches in New Netherland, its extant marriage records do not
begin until 1677. Nevertheless, they provide one of the
most extensive lists of foreign origins for New Netherland
settlers.[50] In the beginning almost all entries consistently give
this information, as well as New Netherland residences as in
the other churches. By 1690 most immigrants had married,
and the entries containing European origins diminish until
they are almost negligible. Some examples of earlier marriage entries follow:

p.6   Betrothed 15 Nov. 1679
Wouter Gysbrechtsz young man from Hilversum in Holland,
residing Breukelen and Lysbeth Jans from Gouda [Holland],
widow of Frans Bloedgoed, residing Vlissingen this country. Married Breukelen with certificate from Vlissingen, 14 December
1679.

p.7   Betrothed 6 June 1680
Carolus Jansz Van Dyk, young man from Amsterdam, Holland,
residing N[ew] Utrecht, Lysbeth Aards Vander Hard, young dame

---

[50] Frank L. Van Cleef, trans., "Baptisms, Marriages and Other Records
from the Reformed Protestant Dutch Church of Flatbush, Kings County,
New York." Copied by Josephine C. Frost, 5 vols. MS. in possession of
the New York Genealogical and Biographical Society; FHL 1016561, it.
2. (Another version of these records in the 1898 *Year Book of the Holland
Society of New York* is unreliable and should not be used.)

from Nieukoop in Holland, residing Midwoud. Married at [New] Utrecht, 27 June 1680.

p.18   Betrothed 18 Nov. 1683
Jan Dirkes Van Vliet, young man from Well in Gelderland and residing at Midwoud and Geertje Verkerkken young dame from Buurmalzen in Gelderland and residing at New Utrecht. Married New Utrecht 2 Nov. [sic, Dec.] 1683.

Early Court and Other Civil Records

One of the most useful sources in locating ancestral homes of seventeenth-century New Netherland settlers is early court and civil records of the colony.

In 1624 when establishing the settlement of New Netherland, the Dutch set up a court of the Governor [Director-General] and his Council which heard all cases, and appeal was only to the West India Company's chamber in Amsterdam. Later lower courts were established in some local jurisdictions with appeal to the Director-General and Council.

In 1653 there was established in the city of New Amsterdam a court made up of city officials, two burgomasters and five schepens. The city's prosecuting officer was known as "the schout." Appeal was still to the Governor-Council. This court formed a prototype for others in the colony.

After the English conquest of 1664 these courts were largely replaced by a system conforming to English practice.

As these colonial New Netherland ancestors were quick to sue on the slightest provocation, the court records for this period are voluminous, and even the most obscure persons may be mentioned. The records covering the longest period of time, and, therefore, the most productive for genealogical research, are those of the Provincial Secretary and the Council in the first five volumes of the *New York Historical Manuscripts: Dutch.*

The first three volumes contain the *Register of the Provincial Secretary, 1638-1660.*[51] The provincial secretary was responsible for recording all of the Council proceedings and maintaining the archives for future reference. For a comprehensive look at the contents of these records, refer to the introduction:

> The *Register of the Provincial Secretary* contain court depositions and agreements which had to be filed with the Secretary [e.g. conveyances, powers of attorney, marriage contracts, building contracts, wills and inventories, and bills of sale].[52]

Moreover, the records include pertinent genealogical data, such as lists of indentures and ship passenger lists, to say nothing of the references to many individuals which identify places of residence in Europe and New Netherland, ages, occupations, relationships, and a host of miscellaneous details.

The author was extremely fortunate to locate in these records two powers of attorney from Egbert van Borsum to his brother Cornelis van Borsum in Amsterdam which provide invaluable information concerning the family. He signed both documents with his mark. The first power of attorney was made 8 July 1644:

> Egbert van Borsum, skipper of the yacht "Prins Willem," . . . appoints and empowers. . . Cornelis van Borsum,. . . brother, residing at Amsterdam, to demand and receive in his name from [his] . . . guardians all such effects as belong to him by inheritance from his deceased father, named [J]an van Bor[sum, and] his deceased mother named Jannitje [A]rents, in their lifetime residing at Emden [Ostfriesland], and as remain in the custody of his

---

[51] Arnold J.F. van Laer, trans., *New York Historical Manuscripts: Dutch, Register of the Provincial Secretary, 1638-1660*, vols. 1-3, ed. Kenneth Scott and Kenn Stryker-Rodda (Baltimore: Genealogical Publishing Co., 1974).

[52] Ibid., xiv.

aforesaid guardians.[53]

The second power of attorney was made 2 August 1647:

> Egbert van Borsum, master of the yacht "Prins Willem," . . .
> appoints and empowers . . . his brother Cornelis van Borsum, mir-
> ror maker, residing in the sign of the Gilded Mirror on Egelan-
> tier's canal at Amsterdam, to ask, demand and collect from the
> honorable directors of the Chartered West India Company,
> chamber of Amsterdam, the sum of seven hundred and forty-
> seven guilders, eighteen stivers, eight pennies, as appears by the
> Book of Monthly Wages, No. F, and the annexed account, which
> above mentioned sum the principal earned of the said directors
> in New Netherland.[54]

These legal documents give direct evidence Egbert van
Borsum, skipper of the yacht "Prins Willem," was in Fort
Amsterdam 8 July 1644 and 2 August 1647. He had a
brother Cornelis van Borsum, mirror maker, living in
Amsterdam at the sign of the Gilded Mirror on Egelantier's
Canal. His father, Jan van Borsum, and his mother, Jannetje
Arents, residing during their lives at Emden, were now
deceased. Egbert van Borsum received an inheritance from
his parents' estate which was still in the hands of his guardians. He signed legal documents with his mark, and, therefore, it is safe to assume he could neither read nor write.

The *Council Minutes* are listed as volumes 4 and 5 of the
New York Historical Manuscripts: Dutch. As stated in the
introduction to volume 1:

> The Council Minutes are a record of executive, legislative,
> and judicial activities. The Council created laws and assisted the
> Director-General in carrying them out. It also served as a judicial
> panel, hearing all cases in which capital punishment could be
> invoked and reviewing decisions of lower courts on appeal, as well

---

[53] Ibid., 2: 238-39.

[54] Ibid., 2: 452-53.

as serving as the local court for the New Amsterdam area.[55]

Some abstracts from the Council Minutes giving places of origin are included:

On the 27th of May Anno 1638
The fiscal, plaintiff, vs. Jan Dircksen from Hamb[urg], defendant, for having traded in furs contrary to his oath.[56]

On the 30th of September, being Thursday
The director and Council of New Netherland having seen the criminal action and demand of the fiscal against Jan Gysbertsen from Rotterdam, charged with manslaughter.[57]

On the 20th of October
Tomas Sandersen, smith, plaintiff, vs. Willem Hendricksz from Wesep [an old form of Weesp, a city 8.5 miles S.E. of Amsterdam], defendant.[58]

On the [3rd] of November Anno 1639
Tonis Cray from Venlo, plaintiff, vs. Gysbert Opdyck, defendant.[59]

On the 14th of March 1641
The director and council of New Netherland have seen the criminal proceeding by Cornelis vander Hoykens, fiscal, plaintiff, against Uldrich Lupholt from Staden, in the diocese of Bremen,

---

[55] Arnold J.F. van Laer, trans., New York Historical Manuscripts: Dutch, vol. 4, Council Minutes, 1638-1649, ed. Kenneth Scott and Kenn Stryker-Rodda (Baltimore: Genealogical Publishing Co., 1974).

Charles T. Gehring, trans. and ed. vol. 5, Council Minutes, 1652-1654 (Baltimore: Genealogical Publishing Co., 1983); n.m. [Dr. Gehring is preparing vol. 6 for publication.]

[56] Ibid., 4: 9.

[57] Ibid., 4: 24.

[58] Ibid., 4: 64.

[59] Ibid., 4: 65.

formerly councillor and commissary of store goods here, defendant.[60]

On the 28th of August 1642
Tomas Smith, plaintiff, vs. Jan Pietersz from Amsterdam, defendant. The plaintiff demands a gun which the defendant is ordered to bring to the courtyard within the Fort and thereupon they are to settle their account.[61]

On the 17th of October [1642]
Claes Eversen from Amsterdam, aged 22 years, says that Jan van Meppelen five or six weeks ago came to the house of Jannitjen Martens.[62]

Another New Netherland civil entity whose records may provide the basis for European research is the Orphanmasters, which were appointed in 1656 to oversee the inheritance of minors. The earliest of their records were published as *The Minutes of the Orphanmasters of New Amsterdam, 1655 - 1663*, as translated by Berthold Fernow.[63] A continuation of these records was published in a small paperback entitled *The Minutes of the Orphanmasters of New Amsterdam 1663 - 1668*, translated by O'Callaghan.[64]

Abstracts of his translation of the same records were also published in the 1900 *Year Book of the Holland Society of New York* along with other Dutch documents and a consoli-

---

[60] Ibid., 4: 103.

[61] Ibid., 4: 157.

[62] Ibid., 4: 167.

[63] Berthold Fernow, trans. and ed., *The Minutes of the Orphanmasters of New Amsterdam, 1655-1663*, 2 vols. (New York: Francis P. Harper, 1902-1907); not in FHL.

[64] E. B. O'Callaghan, trans., *The Minutes of the Orphanmasters of New Amsterdam, 1663-1668*, ed. Kenn Stryker-Rodda and Kenneth Scott (Baltimore: Genealogical Publishing Co., 1976); n.m.

dated name index.[65]

A few entries from the latter are included for the reader's edification:

> 9 Nov. 1655. Meeting of Burgomasters in their quality of orphanmasters when the following matters were treated: . . . Claes Willemsz De Jonge of Amsterdam died at New Amsterdam at the house of Adriaen Blommaert. Inventory taken by Schelluyne.[66]

> 11 May 1657. Jan Corn. Van Rotterdam had been killed in the Indian uprising of 1643. On 11 May 1657, Claes Carstens of Sant in Norway, 50 years old, Evert Duyckingh of Boocken, 36 years, and Isaac Kip of Amsterdam, 30 years, declare that three minor children of said Jan Corn. are living at New Amsterdam.[67]

> 21 June 1659. Saturday. Aaltje Bickers was widow of Gerrit Bickers. He had one child before he married her, which he left in the orphans court at Amsterdam, Holland 1650.[68]

> 15 Dec. 1661. Cornelis Jansz Pluyvier and Geertruyd Andriesz Van Koesvelt made joint will on 5 Sept. 1656 before Notary Segar Van der Pulle, notary at Haarlem in Holland. She was sick in bed at the time. His father was Jan Janse Pluvier. She had a brother. No children mentioned.[69]

Other legal records of New Amsterdam that are useful for establishing places of origin are the registers of the notaries public Salomon Lachaire and Walewyn van der Veen. Unfortunately, they cover only a few years. As stated

---

[65] E.B. O'Callaghan, trans., "Dutch Records in the City Clerk's Office, New York." Extracts from Dutch documents bound in a book labeled "Original Records of Burgomasters and Orphan Masters." *HSYB* 1900: 111-18; FHL 0908989, it. 4.

[66] Ibid., p. 111.

[67] Ibid., p. 113.

[68] Ibid., p. 117.

[69] Ibid., p. 121.

in the introduction to *The Register of Salomon Lachaire*, the notary public played an important role in the legal system of the Dutch period:

> Under Roman Law and its modifications in most countries of continental Europe, the Notary Public is a high   official of the courts of law . . . ; a document, sworn to before a Notary, need not be verified by any court; a last will and testament, drawn up, signed and witnessed before and by a Notary, if left with him, needs no action by a Surrogate (except it be contested).

Regarding the scope of these records the introduction goes on to say:

> Such items are recorded as contracts (including many for building), conveyances, bills of sale, leases, partnership agreements, powers of attorney, depositions, affidavits, petitions, protests, acknowledgements of debt, indentures, apprenticeships, wills, settlements of estate, inventories, bonds, accounts, and translations from and into English. . . .
>
> In his pages appear persons of many nationalities: Dutch, English, Scandinavian, French, Jewish, Indian, and Negro (both slave and free).[70]

Examples from *The Register of Salomon Lachaire* follow, the first and the last translated from the Dutch:

> [10 May 1662]. Reciprocal will between Servyn Lourens van Roodschilt in Denmark, lawful husband, and Tryntie Reynderts van Hengelen in the county of Zutphen, last widow of the late Arent Theunisen van Hengelen: The longest liver of both of them, the full possession and propriety of all the testator's or testatrix's goods, except the bare portion of the testatrix's children by a former marriage, named Reinier, Mary, and Hendrick Arents, and

---

[70] E.B. O'Callaghan, trans., *New York Historical Manuscripts: Dutch, The Register of Salomon Lachaire, Notary Public of New Amsterdam, 1661-1662*, ed. Kenneth Scott and Kenn Stryker-Rodda (Baltimore: Genealogical Publishing Co., 1978), p. xi; n.m.

their child or children. . . .[71]

[13 July 1662]. Appeared before mee Salomon Lachaire, Publicq notary, admitted, etc. and Afore the hereafter named Wittenesses John Houward badseler [bachelor] of Salsberry in Englandt and heas bound him self for the space of one year beginning this daye, to be a tru and faitful servant unto his master tobias feake of flushinge uppon longe Eyslant for to worke uppon his farm . . .[72]

[26 August 1662]. Before me Salomon Lachaire, Notary Public, admitted, etc., and before the undernamed witnesses, appeared the worthy Harmen Tomassen from Amesfoort, master shoe-maker, residing in the village of Beverwyck at Fort Orange in New Netherland, as husband and guardian of Catelyntie Berck, last widow of the late Dirck Bensingh, and in that quality co-heir of the late Tamson Berck and his wife, the appearer's wife's father and mother deceased, in their lifetime inhabitants of, and having died in the City of Amsterdam in Holland . . . .[73]

The records of Walewyn Van der Veen, Notary Public, 1662-1664, contain essentially the same type of material as that of Salomon Lachaire. However, it is important to be aware of two translations of Van der Veen. One was made about 1860 by O'Callaghan but never published. However, abstracts are included in the 1900 *Year Book of the Holland Society of New York*. The other is a translation by Fernow published in volume 2 of *Minutes of the Orphanmasters Court*, already referenced.

Comparing the entries in these two translations the genealogical information is almost identical. However, the spelling of names and places frequently disagrees, emphasiz-ing the difficulty in reading the handwriting. Of course, the abstract contains only pertinent matter. In the interest of brevity the O'Callaghan version will be used here:

---

[71] Ibid., p. 155.

[72] Ibid., p. 172.

[73] Ibid., p. 189.

4 Sept. 1662. Cornelis Van Langevelde, as husband and legal guardian of his wife, Maritie Jansen, daughter and heiress of Jan Cornelissen dec'd, of Rotterdam, *alias* Joncker, who had been murdered by the Indians in 1643, appoints as attorney Andries Jeremiassen Spieringh, merchant, about to depart for Holland. In said capacity said Spieringh will demand and collect whatever is due to deceased's estate from Cornelis Pieters Willemsen, residing in the village of Goudriaan, near Thienhoven, in the Alblasserwaert, brother-in-law of the aforesaid Jan Cornelisen of Rotterdam, and from Grietje Adriaensen, widow of Adriaen Cornelissen Joncker, widow of the brother of said Jan Cornelissen, living near Gorkum, in the hamlet named the Haes. Witnesses, Jacobus Van de Water, Claes Van Elslant.[74]

28 Feb. 1664. Adriaen Hegeman of Long Island, as husband of Catharine Margits, confers powers of attorney upon Joseph Margits, of Amsterdam, Holland, his father-in-law, to collect inheritance for his wife, coming to her from her late brother, Joseph Margits who died in the East Indies. Witnesses, Hendrick Bosch, Thomas Lambersen.[75]

. . . June 1664. Jan Roelofsen confers powers of attorney upon Frederyck Jeronnimus, his father-in-law, residing at Amsterdam, Holland, for the purpose of receiving inheritance left to him by his father Roelof Luykassen, decd., and his mother Aeltie Hermanssen, also deceased, within the city of Ootmarssen, in the province of Overyssel. Has also a brother William Roelofsen living at Ootmarssum. Witnesses, Hendrick Bosch, Jan Gerritsen Van Buytenhuysen.[76]

Proceeding up the Hudson River, the court records of the Manor of Rensselaerswyck can also be of value. The records of this court are published under the title *Minutes of the Court of Rensselaerswyck, 1648-1652*. In the preface Van Laer says:

---

[74] E. B. O'Callaghan, trans., "Walewyn Van der Veen's Record, 1662-1664," HSYB 1900: 152-58; FHL 0908989, it. 4.

[75] Ibid., p. 158.

[76] Ibid.

The court of the colony Rensselaerswyck, . . . formed from an early date an important part of the judicial organization of the province of New Netherland. The court was erected by Kiliaen van Rensselaer by virtue of the power conferred upon him by the charter of Freedoms and Exemptions of 1629, which provided that members of the Dutch West India Company who within four years after giving notice to the company should plant in New Netherland a colony of fifty adults should be acknowledged as patroons [Dutch for patrons or lords] and should hold their land from the company as a perpetual fief of inheritance, with 'high, middle and low jurisdiction.' By these terms the patroons were authorized to administer civil and criminal justice, in person or by deputy, within the limits of their respective colonies and to erect courts whose jurisdiction should extend to matters affecting life and limb, although article 20 of the charter provided that from all judgments given by the courts of the patroons above 50 guilders there should be appeal to the director general and Council of New Netherland.[77]

As in other early court records of New Netherland, *Minutes of the Court of Rensselaerswyck* are replete with references to settlers' places of origin, for example:

Thursday, 7 May Anno 1648
The honorable director, plaintiff, against Hans Jansz from Rotterdam, for having beaten an Indian. First default.[78]

[25 v] 23 February Anno 1649
Evert Pels from Steltyn [Stettin, Germany, now in Poland], by this his signature becomes surety and bail for Jacob Aertsz, waegenaer. . . . Done this 25th of February Anno 1649.[79]

[85 v] Extraordinary session, 6 September 1651
As to the question which has arisen between Pieter Bronck

---

[77] Arnold J.F. van Laer, trans. and ed., *Minutes of the Court of Rensselaerswyck, 1648-1652* (Albany: University of the State of New York, 1922), p. 7; FHL 1321474, it. 10.

[78] Ibid., p. 29.

[79] Ibid., p. 65.

and Joost Teunisz from Norden. . . .[80]

For research concerning the European origins of other ancestors in this area, the reader is referred to the new translation of the *Fort Orange Court Minutes, 1652-1660*. In the introduction a large section has been extracted from Van Laer's preface to his earlier translation of these minutes. Only a small, applicable portion is repeated here:

> The jurisdiction of the court comprised Fort Orange, the village of Beverwijck, Schenectady, Kinderhook, Claverack, Coxsackie, Catskill, and, until 16 May 1661, when a court was established at the Esopus. Excluded from the jurisdiction was the colony of Rensselaerswijck, which maintained its own court, side by side with that of Fort Orange and the village of Beverwijck until 1665, when by order of Governor Richard Nicolls the two courts were consolidated.[81]

An unusual find made in these court records was a very early civil marriage which is not likely to be found elsewhere and also supplies places of origin for those involved:

[9] Extraordinary Session, ultimo May 1652
    Adriaen Jansz van Leyden, aged 25 years, and Maeriecke Rijverdinxs van Dansick [Danzig, now Gdansk, Poland], aged 24 years, having requested to enter the married state, permission is granted to have the first proclamation of the banns take place on Sunday next.[82]

[12] Ordinary Session, 18 June 1652
    This day Adriaen Jansz from Leyden and Maria Reverdinghs van Danswijck were united in marriage before the court here.[83]

---

[80] Ibid., p. 159.

[81] Charles T. Gehring, trans. and ed., *Fort Orange Court Minutes, 1652-1660* (Syracuse: Syracuse University Press, 1990), p. xxvi; n.m.

[82] Ibid., p. 11.

[83] Ibid., p. 14.

Another set of records for the Albany area providing many places of origin for New Netherland settlers is *Early Records of the City and County of Albany and Colony of Rensselaerswyck*, particularly volume 3 of this series, containing notarial records. An excellent treatise on these records and the office of notary is included in the preface to this volume:

> The two volumes of Notarial Papers in the Albany county clerk's office which are published herewith belong to a class of records of which, considering the number of Dutch notaries who are known to have practised their profession in this State, comparatively little has been preserved. Corresponding in character to the well-known registers of notaries Salomon La Chair and Walewyn van der Veen in New York City, these Notarial Papers consist of the originals, or "minutes" of a variety of legal instruments, such as bonds, powers of attorney, contracts and bills of sale, indentures of service, assignments, leases, wills, marriage settlements and inventories of estates, which were executed before notaries Dirck van Schelluyne, Adriaen Jansen van Ilpendam and Jan Juriaensen Becker.[84]

Only a few examples from these records, showing the wealth of material providing places of origin, can be covered here:

Will of Daniel Ringout
　　On this day, the 29th of August 1662 . . . personally came and appeared before me, Dirck van Schelluyne, notary public . . . Daniel Rinchout, elderly bachelor, born in the land of Pomeren [Pomerania, Germany], about 36 years of age (as he declared), dwelling in the village of Beverwyck in New Netherland. . . .
　　He does nominate . . . his brother, Jan Rinchout (who with his wife and family is dwelling in the testator's house here), to be

---

[84] Arnold J.F. van Laer, ed., *Notarial Papers 1 and 2, 1660-1696*. Vol. 3 of Jonathan Pearson, trans. *Early Records of the City and County of Albany and Colony of Rensselaerswyck*, 4 vols. (Albany: University of the State of New York, 1869-1919), p. 3; FHL 0924661, it. 2. Note: A new edition of these notarial papers is being prepared by the New Netherland Project.

his sole and universal heir. . . . [Brother Aertman Rinchout, dwelling in Pomeren, mentioned but not heard from for eight years, so he may not be alive].[85]

Will of Eldert Gerbertsen Cruyff and his wife
     On this day the 3d of July 1663, before me, Dirck van Schelluyne, notary public . . . personally came and appeared. . . . Eldert Gerbertsz Cruyff, born in Hilleverson in Gooylant in the Netherlands, dwelling in the colony of Rensselaerswyck, and Tryntie Jans, born at Noorstrant in Oostlant his wife. . . The testatrix's son, named Albert Janssz Ryckman, son of Jan Janssz Ryckman, her first husband, deceased, [to be provided for].[86]

Will of Marten Cornelissen from Ysselsteyn and his wife Maeycke Cornelis from Barrevelt
     In the year . . . 1676-7, on the 12th day of the month of January, before me, Adriaen van Ilpendam, notary public . . . came and appeared . . . Maerten Cornelisz, born in the city of Ysselsteyn, and his wife Maeycke Cornelis, born at Barrevelt, both dwelling at the Claverrack . . . [mentions children not named].[87]

The court at the Esopus,[88] now Kingston, Ulster County, will be the last discussed. According to Peter R. Christoph's introduction to the *Kingston Papers*:

     At first the Esopus fell under the jurisdiction of the court of Fort Orange and Beverwyck. Management of public affairs became the responsibility of the military commander at the garrison after the erection of the palisaded village in 1658. The residents desired a local civil administration, and in response to their request the directors of the Amsterdam Chamber of the

---

[85] Ibid., pp. 181-82.

[86] Ibid., pp. 219-20.

[87] Ibid., pp. 359-60.

[88] Esopus: From an Algonquin word meaning "creek." Applied at various times to a variety of streams including both the present Esopus and Rondout creeks. Later applied to the general region and for a time to the village of Kingston.

Dutch West India Company made the Esopus an independent
jurisdiction, . . . and instructed Director-General Stuyvesant to
organize a court. Stuyvesant resisted the order, but after being
censured for his recalcitrance, he issued an ordinance on 16 May
1661, establishing the court.[89]

Additional information is added concerning the contents
of its records:

> The court minutes are a record of the hearings and trials,
> 1661-1684. The secretary's papers contain copies of legal trans-
> actions (contracts, agreements, bonds, wills, and powers of attor-
> ney) and transfers of real estate for the period 1664-1681. Prior
> to 1664 no separate secretarial record seems to have been kept,
> a few deeds and mortgages being entered in the first volume of
> court minutes. All the existing records were deposited in the
> Ulster County Clerk's office on 16 December 1686.[90]

As to the research value of these court records:

> The genealogist will find a wealth of material here . . . : wills,
> baptisms, marriages, orphan records, and frequent mention of
> family relationships in passing.[91]

A few examples of this significant material are given,
including (as in the court records of Fort Orange) a registration of civil marriage banns and a baptism not found in the
records of the Kingston Dutch Church:

> This 7 December 1672, William Fisher had his banns
> registered with Jannetie Crafford of Amsterdam which banns shall
> be publicly announced in the church tomorrow.

---

[89] Dingman Versteeg, trans., *New York Historical Manuscripts: Dutch,
Kingston Papers, 1661-1675*, 2 vols., ed. Peter R. Christoph, Kenneth Scott,
and Kenn Stryker-Rodda (Baltimore: Genealogical Publishing Co., 1976),
1: xii-xiii; n.m.

[90] Ibid., 1: xv.

[91] Ibid., 1: xxi.

Same date, Thoomas Teunesen Quick, born at New York and Rynbregh Jurriaensen, born at Kingston.[92]

This 14 December 1672, Hendrick Jansen, young man, born at Beest in Gelderland, and Catharina Hansen, born at New York, had their banns registered.[93]

A single undated entry found between entries dated 21 May and 21 August 1673:

Baptized the child of Arent Teunesen, named Teunes.[94]

Again, as in the preceding records, wills provide the largest number of references to European origins of original settlers in *The Kingston Papers*:

> Before me, Mattheus Capito, Secretary of the village of Wildwyck . . . there appeared . . . Albert Gerretsen from Embderland [Emden, Germany] . . . And further . . . disposes and wills that his lawful wife Willemtje Jacobs . . . Dated 3 September 1665.
> (Signed) Albert Gerretsen.[95]

One will is of special interest to the author, that of an ancestor Matthew Blanchan, already mentioned in the passenger lists and marriage records of the Kingston Dutch Church. An abstract follows:

> . . . before me, Mattheus Capito, . . . there appeared . . . the worthy Mattheu Blanchan, born in the village of Noeuville o corne in the parish Ricame de la conté de St.Paul in the province of Artois [now Departement Pas de Calais, France]. . . . Magdalen Joire his lawful wife, shall possess the whole estate 'here in

---

[92] Ibid., 2: 489.

[93] Ibid.

[94] Ibid., 2: 739.

[95] Ibid., 2: 575.

America, as long as she remains a widow' also 'all the land in
Artois where the testator was born and in Armentères and other
places'. . . . Minor children Magdelena, Elisabeth, and Mattheu,
and married daughters Catharinen and Marien. . . . Done at
Wildwyck in America this 7/17 September 1665. (Signed) Mattheu
Blanchan.[96]

Using this will with passenger lists and church records,
the exact parish in France from which the Blanchan family
emigrated was determined and located on a current map.
Unfortunately, extant parish registers do not begin until
1737. However, by also searching the records of the Roman
Catholic Church of Armentères, the marriage of Matthew
Blanchan and Magdalena Joire was located and the baptismal record of an additional child, before unknown, to be
fully referenced later. Since Armentères was the birthplace
of Magdalena Joire, her baptism and those of her siblings
were recorded in the parish. From there the author was able
to follow the flight of this Huguenot family through England,
Germany, and the Netherlands to America in search of
religious freedom.

Several very helpful research aids are found in the appendixes of volume 2 of this set of court records:

Appendix C: Glossary: Included in this list are Dutch and Indian
Words, odd and archaic usages of English terms, place names,
governmental and military offices, legal terms, and definitions of
court and social practices.

Appendix E: Former Dutch Coins, Weights and Measures, and
Their Equivalents: Numerous coins, weights, and measures are
mentioned in the Kingston records, many of them undoubtedly
unfamiliar to either the general reader or the historian.[97]

Many other seventeenth-century civil records exist which
either give only a few places of origin for early settlers of

---

[96] Ibid., 2: 575-76.

[97] Ibid., 2: 755-61; 763-66.

New Netherland or none at all, e.g. *The Records of New Amsterdam*.[98] These will not be discussed here, but it may be advisable to at least check their indexes for the ancestor, as well as for possible relatives.

If the place of origin has not been located in New Netherland passenger lists, church records, or civil records, the researcher must rely on European records to supply the needed information. This will be the subject of chapter 2.

---

[98] Berthold Fernow, trans., *The Records of New Amsterdam from 1653 - 1674*, 7 vols., 1897. Reprint. Baltimore: Genealogical Publishing Co., 1976.

2 USING EUROPEAN RECORDS TO ESTABLISH THE PLACE OF ORIGIN

Preliminary Searches in Amsterdam

Since most passengers to New Netherland sailed from Amsterdam, this is the first place to search in the Netherlands. The author has found from experience that many of those who went through that city were refugees from the Spanish Netherlands or Germany. Others were natives of the Netherlands who came to the thriving metropolis to work while awaiting sponsors to New Netherland. Here many married, and some had children baptized. So Amsterdam is an excellent place to start seventeenth-century European research regardless of the ultimate place of origin.

Fortunately Hendrik O. Slok prepared a research paper for the Family History Library on *Church and Civil Records of Amsterdam, the Netherlands, before 1811*. It has become the author's "constant companion." Along with a brief historical outline, the paper includes a commentary on church and civil records, and the indexes to them (with Family History Library film numbers). Slok describes the indexes thus:

> To increase the accessibility of information in the numerous church and civil registers of pre-1811 Amsterdam, card indexes have been prepared to include names from all records. Civil records and approximately sixty congregations of a dozen denominations are represented in these master indexes. The indexes are in the Amsterdam Municipal Archives, and a copy is on microfilm at the [Family History Library].[1]

---

[1] *Church and Civil Records of Amsterdam, the Netherlands before 1811*, FHL C: 25. (Part of a series, *Genealogical Research Papers for the Netherlands*, by the Family History Library), listed following chapter 3; MF 6000355-6, p. 53.

This statement is somewhat misleading, as the paper also mentions various records, both church and civil, which are not indexed. Some are available at the Family History Library on microfilm or in book form, while others can only be used at the Amsterdam Municipal Archives (Gemeente Archief). For information on the latter write the archives:

Gemeentelijke Archiefdienst van Amsterdam
Amsteldijk 67
1074 HZ Amsterdam
The Netherlands

The following indexes which are available on microfilm at the Family History Library and through the family history centers are listed by their call numbers in Slok's paper:

1. Baptisms, all churches, 1564-1700, by given names.

2. Baptisms, all churches, 1564-1811, by surnames.

3. Marriage intentions, 1578-1811, by patronymics and surnames.

4. Burials, 1553-1700, by given names plus patronymics.

5. Burials, 1553-1650, by patronymics.

6. Burials, 1553-1811, by surnames.[2]

He explains very clearly how to use each of the above indexes and gives the number and contents of each reel of film.

Slok does not mention a third index to baptisms by patronymics. This can also be very useful, if either the patronymic of the father or the mother is found in the ancestor's baptismal record or marriage intention. In the patronymic index there should be a card for each parent with a patronymic, doubling the researcher's opportunity to obtain

---

[2] Ibid., pp. 62-70.

all of an ancestor's siblings.   This index can be obtained from
the Family History Library Catalog under "Netherlands,
Noord-Holland, Amsterdam--Church Records," then "Amsterdam (Noord-Holland),   Gemeente Archief 2," and finally
"Fiches collectie van dopen onder patronym" (index card
collection of baptisms by patronymics). An example of how
one baptism is listed in the patronymic index follows:

Father's card:

Aertz	Aert	Vader	[father]	1589
Barents	Griette	Moeder	[mother]	Nov 2
	Aert	Kind	[child]	

Mother's Card:

Baerents	Griette	Moeder	[mother]	1589
Aertsz	Aert	Vader	[father]	Nov 2
	Aert	Kind	[child]	

If the reseacher still does not have a place of origin for
the ancestor after searching all records mentioned in chapter
1, and is only tapping into Amsterdam records perchance the
person resided there for a time, the marriage intentions are
by far the most informative. They generally give the town of
origin, or the next highest municipality if the town is small
(although the names are often badly misspelled); the age,
occupation, name of those accompanying the couple, persons
giving permission to marry, former wife or husband if any,
and place of residence in Amsterdam.

Special attention should be given to the fact that there
were two categories of marriage intentions found in Amsterdam -- one the church records (kerk) and the other civil
(pui), which is noted on the upper right side of each card in
the index to marriage intentions. Depending on which category, the film number will be found in Slok's paper under
one of two lists for the "entire city of Amsterdam," church
pages 15-18 and civil pages 42-43.

An example of finding the place of origin in Amsterdam

marriage intentions is that of Coenradt ten Eyck, who came to New Netherland prior to the "passenger lists," and whose origin was not found in later records (See Frontispiece):

> 12 May 1645, Coenradt ten Eyck van Meurs schoenmakergezel wonende 11 jare op de N.Z. Voorburgwall out 27 jaren geen ouders hebben en Maria Boel van Keulen out 23 jaren wonen op de Coninxgracht, geen ouders hebbende geassisteerd met haar zuster Jannetie Boel.
> s/Konradt ten Eyck
> s/Maria Boel
>
> Dese personen zyn tot Amstelveen getrouwtr de 4 June 1645 door Symen Wilmerdonex, prest. aldaar.

Translation

> 12 May 1645, Coenradt ten Eyck from Moers [Nordrhein-Westfalen, Germany, formerly Rheinland, Prussia] shoemaker's helper residing 11 years at the N.Z. Voorburgwal, age 27 years, having no parents [living in Amsterdam]; and Maria Boel from Cologne [same land as Moers], age 23 years, residing at the Koningsgracht, having no parents [living in Amsterdam], accompanied by her sister, Jannetie Boel.
> s/Konradt ten Eyck
> s/Maria Boel
>
> These persons were married at Amstelveen [a small, independent village now a part of Amsterdam] 4 June 1645 by Symen Wilmerdonex, pastor there.[3]

One of the most difficult items to decipher in these marriage intentions is the name of the street or area of Amsterdam where the individuals resided, as there is usually no duplicate word with which to compare it should the film or writing be poor. This problem may be overcome by using A. Margaretha van Gelder's *Amsterdamsche straatnamen: geschiedkundig verklaard* (a street directory of Amsterdam

---

[3] Marriage Intentions of All Churches in Amsterdam, 461: 48; FHL 0113203; REC. 118 (1977): 14.

with maps and history).[4]
Six detailed maps, located at the back of the book, are especially noteworthy. The first shows the entire city with the various areas outlined, then a map of each area follows. Thus, if the street on which the ancestor lived is listed in the book, it is possible to find the exact location and the correct spelling on the applicable map.

If Van Gelder's book is temporarily unavailable in the library, or it is necessary to do the research at a family history center on microfilm, use *Inhoudsopgraaf te Amsterdam over de jaren 1875-1897* (a table of contents to the population registration records of Amsterdam with street names).[5] Although this book is not nearly as useful for the researcher's purpose as Van Gelder, it will generally fill the need.

Using the indexes to baptisms, three children were located for the aforementioned ten Eyck couple in the Dutch Reformed Church records of Amsterdam, the first in the Oudekerk [Old Church], and the last two in the Nieuwekerk [New Church]:

i. Marija, bap. 2 Apr. 1646, wit:
   Hendrik Boel and Marij ten Eyck.
ii. Jacob, bap. 8 Aug 1647, wit: Jacob ten Eyck.
iii. Deryck, bap. 27 Oct. 1648, wit: Mathijs
   Glas, Sijbert van Loon, and Magdalena Ruts.[6]

Special care is required in using the baptismal records of the Nieuwekerk in Amsterdam. Errors can easily be made in reading the dates of baptisms due to the confusing manner

---

[4] A. Margaretha van Gelder, *Amsterdamsche straatnamen: geschiedkundig verklaard* (Amsterdam: P.N. van Kampen & Zoon, 1913); n.m.

[5] Gemeentelijke Archiefdienst Amsterdam, *Inhoudsopgaaf . . . te Amsterdam over de jaren 1875-1897* (Amsterdam: Het Archief, n.d.); FHL 1190174.

[6] REC. 118 (1977): 14-15.

in which the dates are recorded. From 1587 through 1602[7] the date is given, as might be expected, at the beginning of each day's baptisms. Between 1603 and 1705,[8] however, lines drawn in the margin indicate the beginning and end of each day, and the date appears in the margin, usually about halfway between these lines.

Although the Citizen (Poorter) Registers are not indexed, it is not too difficult to find the man in these chronological documents, if he became a citizen when he came to Amsterdam or reached maturity (21 years). Unfortunately, however, there is a gap in the records from 1604 to 1636, a time period that includes many New Netherland ancestors. Slok describes these records thus:

> The earliest extant registers date from 1584. A register entry contains the date of the oath of citizenship, name, trade, former residence, name of official who administered the oath, and reference to the fee paid. Municipal laws required citizenship before a person could conduct a business or trade or hold membership in a guild.[9]

Searching these Citizen Registers an entry was found for "Koenraed ten Eijck van Moeurs, Schoenmaker," who became a burger or citizen of Amsterdam 1 August 1645, several months after his marriage (See Illustration 1).[10]

With the additional information found in the records of Amsterdam, it was possible to trace Coenradt ten Eyck back to his place of origin and find his baptismal record, with also two of his siblings, in the Reformed Church of Moers. In addition the marriage of his parents was located.

---

[7] Baptisms Nieuwekerk of Amsterdam, 1587-1602; FHL 0113143.

[8] Baptisms Nieuwekerk of Amsterdam, 1603-1705; FHL 0113144-48.

[9] Slok, *Records of Amsterdam*; FHL C:25, MF 6000355-356, p.36.

[10] Citizens (Poorter) Registers of Amsterdam, 1584-1652, E: 160, verso; FHL 0114915.

More knowledge concerning the wife's family was gleaned from various church registers in Cologne and led to additional records in Antwerp, Belgium, taking the Boel family back several generations. This information can be found in chapter 4, "Ten Eyck-Boel Family," pages 85-87. This is a very good example of using Amsterdam records to trace an ancestor for whom no place of origin was found in New Netherland records. However, additional information may also be found when an ancestor gives a place of origin in New Netherland records but makes a stop-over in Amsterdam before proceeding to New Netherland. Following the detailed instructions in Slok's paper and the research aids in chapter 3 of this book, success can be had with only a superficial knowledge of the Dutch language.

The Walloon or Leiden Collection

Another extensive collection, helpful in locating records of seventeenth-century New Netherland ancestors, is the famous *Collection des fiches* or *Leiden Collection*, so named because it was the work of the Bibliotheque Wallonne (Walloon[11] Library) in the City of Leiden, the Netherlands.

Slok also prepared a paper covering these records for the Family History Library, entitled *Church Records of the*

---

[11] Walloons and Huguenots: These terms were generally used to designate French Protestants who came to the Netherlands and New Netherland. The natives of northern France and southern Belgium were and still are known as Walloons. The Calvinist movement reached northern France by 1542, spreading from there across Belgium in 1543 and into the Netherlands in 1559. Many Calvinist Walloons who fled to the Netherlands and elsewhere came from Artois and Flanders (now Departements Pas de Calais and Nord). The origin of the name Huguenots is uncertain, but it became a general designation for all who were affiliated with the Protestant Reformation in France.

*Netherlands--Walloon or French Reformed (Waalse of Frans
Hervormde).* He describes the collection thus:

> A commission appointed to compile historical information about
> the Walloon [French Protestant] church began its work in 1875 by
> indexing *most* of the baptismal, marriage, membership, and death
> records of Walloon congregations in the Netherlands for the period
> prior to 1812 [civil registration].
> This project also included registers from many German Walloon
> churches. Further, copies of the church registers of Montauban, La
> Rochelle, Sedan and St. Quentin in France prior to 1685 were
> incorporated into the project. Also, abstracts of French surname
> entries from the Dutch Reformed church records were made at
> random.[12]

Slok goes on to explain the card indexes to this collection:

> Information has been extracted from the parish registers of the
> French Protestant and Dutch Reformed churches and entered in
> abbreviated form on cards that now comprise the [Leiden Collec-
> tion] . . . [currently] housed in the Centraal Bureau voor Genealogie
> in the Hague, but formerly at Leiden. This collection contains
> histories of not only individuals but entire families of refugees who
> later went to such places as South Africa, North and South
> America, and the West Indies. Membership records of Walloons
> residing in England or Germany who visited their relatives in the
> Netherlands are often found, and those who were on their way from
> Germany to England or the Americas are also listed.
> Abstracts from the Walloon church records of England are not
> included in this card index but can be found in the publications of
> the Huguenot Society of London, which are also available at the
> [FHL]. Most of the Walloon records in the Netherlands prior to
> 1812, including the card index, have been microfilmed by the
> [FHL] and are available at the library or through the [family history
> centers].[13]

This paper then lists the Family History Library call

---

[12] *Church Records of the Netherlands--Walloon or French Reformed
(Waalse of Frans Hervormde)*; FHL C: 23, MF 6000055, p. 2.

[13] Ibid.

numbers of the Leiden Collection indexes. Following the indexes is a list of Walloon churches in the Netherlands, and some in France and Germany, which gives the name of the church, the country, type of records, and time period they cover, with their Family History Library call numbers.

A search in the index to the Leiden Collection revealed that the author's Blanchan family resided in Mannheim, Baden-Württemburg, Germany (formerly Mannheim, Baden) before coming with the Dutch West India Company to New Netherland. They attended the Walloon or French Reformed church in Mannheim. The references as translated from the index are:

Baptized at the French Church of Mannheim the 22 Apr. 1655, Mathieu child of Mathieu Blanchan and Magdalena Jore.

Married at Mannheim 10 Oct. 1655, Catherine Blanchan and Louys Duboijs, son of Christian.

Married at Mannheim 31 Jan. 1660, Marie Blanchon and Antoine Crispel.[14]

Unfortunately these early records of the French Reformed Church of Mannheim have not been microfilmed by the Family History Library. For further information about them, contact the Huguenot Historical Society, P.O. Box 339, New Paltz, N.Y. 12561.

Using the Leiden Collection, tracing Walloon ancestors in seventeenth-century Dutch or German parishes becomes a relatively easy task. However, one should also check the indexes of the publications of the Huguenot Society of London.

---

[14] Card Index Bibliotheque Wallonne, Leiden, So. Holland, the Netherlands; FHL 0199909, n.p.

Publications of the Huguenot Society of London

Some of the French-speaking Protestants who eventually
came to New Netherland had been refugees in England. *The
Publications of the Huguenot Society of London*, a series of
volumes begun in 1887, are a major source for these refugees. Before considering the records it will be advisable to
learn something concerning their background and the
circumstances leading to their flight. Francis W. Cross in his
History of the Walloon and Huguenot Church at Canterbury
says:

> The registers of the Walloon Church at Canterbury give the places
> of origin of the members who were married in the Crypt after July
> 1590. Between that date and July 1627 one thousand individuals
> are described as born out of England. . . . A large majority of the
> thousand alien-born members came from a line of towns and villag-
> es situated within a few miles of the present frontier of France and
> Belgium, and for the most part within the province of French Flan-
> ders. . . . In smaller numbers the refugees came from all parts of
> French Flanders, Artois, and Picardy, especially from the districts
> of Arras, Amiens, and Calais; but the chief home of the Walloons
> who took refuge at Canterbury was the borderland stretching from
> Armentères to Valenciennes.[15]

Cross goes on to say:

> It was upon this part of the Spanish Netherlands that the storm of
> persecution first fell. The country was then esteemed one of the
> richest in Europe, and its towns were hives of industry whose looms
> produced the finest fabrics of wool and linen. . . . Into their country,
> at the close of the year 1566, the Spanish [troops] were sent to wipe
> out the Reformation. . . . The persecution raged throughout Flan-
> ders and Artois, and thousands in despair began their perilous exo-

---

[15] Francis William Cross, *History of the Walloon and Huguenot Church
at Canterbury*, The Publications of the Huguenot Society of London, vol.
15 (Canterbury: Cross & Jackman, 1898), pp. 24-25; FHL 0962136, it. 3.

dus.[16]

Among the most useful volumes in this series are *The Registers of the Walloon or Strangers' Church in Canterbury* which contain a wealth of genealogical material.[17] The only reference found anywhere to the earliest identifiable Blanchan ancestors is in a marriage contract between Antoine Blanchan and Martinne Valque which states (as translated):

> 12 April 1649. Marriage Contract between Antoine BLANCHAMP [BLANCHANT], son of the late Leonin, and the late Isabeau le Roy, his father and mother, assisted by Mathieu Blanchamp [Blanchan], his brother; and Martinne VALQUE, daughter of Jacques, assisted by Jaque Valque [Valke], her brother, and Mathieu Marhem. Mention is made of land in Arthois belonging to the said Anthoine. Witness, A. Denis. (Vol. iv., No. 157).[18]

Mathieu Blanchan also had a child baptized in the same church:

> 16 May 1647 Magdelaine, daughter of Mathieu Blanchan and Magdelaine Joore. Wit: Pierre Lambert, Jacques Toulet, Magdelaine Deschamps, Magdelaine Pruuno.[19]

Another useful source published by the The Huguenot Society of London is William John Charles Moens' *The Walloons and Their Church at Norwich; Their History and*

---

[16] Ibid.

[17] Robert Hovenden, ed., *The Registers of the Walloon or Strangers' Church in Canterbury*, The Publications of the Huguenot Society of London, vol. 5, pts. 1-3 (Lymington, Eng.: C.T. King, 1891-1898); FHL 0086956-7, hereafter WCC.

[18] WCC 2: 725.

[19] WCC 1: 209.

Registers, 1565-1832.[20] Although the author did not find any reference to specific ancestors in these records, the name Crespel, later of New York, was found as early as 1596 under many spellings, such as Crepel, Creper, Crespelle, Chrespel, Crespieul and Cresepel, indicating the Crespel family came through Norwich.

Samuel Smiles in *The Huguenots, Their Settlements, Churches, and Industries in England and Ireland*, supplies a good understanding of why these refugees from the Spanish Inquisition became dissatisfied with the home they found in England and were again on the move:

> The utmost concession that the King would grant was, that those who were born aliens might still enjoy the use of their own church service; but that all their children born in England should regularly attend the parish churches. Even this small concession was limited only to the congregation at Canterbury, and measures were taken to enforce conformity in the other dioceses.
>
> The refugees thus found themselves exposed to anglican persecution, instead of a Papal one. Rather than endure it, several thousands of them left the country, abandoning their new homes, and again risking the loss of everything, in preference to giving up their views as to religion. About a hundred and forty families emigrated from Norwich into Holland. . . .[21]

With this information in mind it seems logical to also check the Anglican parish church records in London or any other English town where the Walloon ancestor may have resided during the sixteenth or seventeenth century.

---

[20] William John Charles Moens, *The Walloons and Their Church at Norwich; Their History and Registers, 1565-1832*, The Publications of the Huguenot Society of London, vol. 1 (Lymington, Eng.: R.E. King and C. King, 1887-1888); FHL 0599301, it. 3.

[21] Samuel Smiles, *The Huguenots, Their Settlements, Churches, and Industries in England and Ireland*, 6th ed. (London: John Murray, 1889), p. 129; FHL 1426146, it. 2.

3 USING DUTCH RESEARCH AIDS

Gazetteers, Maps, and Research Papers

After obtaining the name of the ancestor's place of origin, the researcher may try locating the place and become more confused than ever! It is possible the place name was written by a clerk totally unfamiliar with the area, causing a badly distorted spelling. The correct spelling *must be found*. This problem requires the use of a good gazetteer (index to place names). In the author's opinion, the best gazetteer for the Netherlands is the one most frequently used at the Family History Library for Dutch and Belgian research, the *Aardrijkskundig woordenboek der Nederlanden*.[1] This is a gazetteer of the localities in the present-day Netherlands as well as Belgium, Luxembourg, and the East Indies (now Indonesia), all formerly a part of the Netherlands. Of course, this set of books is written in Dutch, as are most Dutch research aids. Therefore, it will be necessary to consult a good Dutch-English dictionary. This is often quite sufficient for understanding a gazetteer. The author recommends the *Dutch-English, English-Dutch Van Goor Dictionary*.[2]

If all else fails, it will be necessary to find someone with a good knowledge of the language to assist in reading the specific entry once found. Probably this person will even recognize the correct spelling of the place at a glance.

When there is no one in the area fluent in Dutch, the

---

[1] Abraham Jacobus van der Aa, comp., *Aardrijkskundig woordenboek der Nederlanden*, 14 vols. (Gorinchem: Jacobus Noorduyn en Zoon, 1839-51. Reprint. 1979); FHL 0496582, it. 2.

[2] G. B. Van Goor, *Dutch-English, English-Dutch Van Goor Dictionary* (s'Gravenhage: G. B. Van Goor, 1938); FHL 1183584, it. 2.

author suggests a week's "genealogical vacation" at the Family History Library, where there is a Dutch Research Consultant on duty at the International Reference Desk. Should the research lead to other countries, there are consultants equally fluent in most European languages. The reader can then do the research, saving money in the long run. Once the correct place is ascertained, almost all extant Dutch Church records, as well as many other types of records, are available on microfilm and can be used at any family history center throughout the country.

Another source for determining correct spelling and learning more about a place is an encyclopedia. The author uses the *Encyclopaedia Britannica*, if the town or area is large enough to be included. This encyclopedia is usually found in most public and school libraries and greatly enhances one's knowledge. Best of all, it is in English!

The next step is to locate the place on a current map. For this purpose the author uses two research aids. The first is a good auto atlas of Europe, of which there are several. The author recommends *Der Grosse Conti Auto-Atlas*.[3] This is a detailed atlas of Europe, including city maps. The second is *Gemeente-Atlas van Nederland: naar officieele bronnen bewerkt*, a detailed atlas of the Netherlands showing town and province jurisdictions.[4]

Using a good gazetteer and a current detailed map, the next step is to determine the *jurisdictions* which generated records for the place of origin. All European countries are organized by jurisdictions similar to the United States, e.g. the town, county, and state. All localities are listed in the Family History Library Catalog by their modern location (except Germany for which the pre-1918 boundaries are used) under first the country, then the state or its equivalent

---

[3] *Der Grosse Conti Auto-Atlas* (Munich: JRO Kartografische Verlagsgesellschaft, 1983).

[4] J. Kuyper, *Gemeente-Atlas van Nederland: naar officieele bronnen bewerkt*, 11 vols. (Leeuwarden: Hugo Suringar, 1955); FHL 1181567.

(province, etc.), then the county, and last the town. The first several fiche at the beginning of each country listed in the locality file of the Family History Library Catalog provide an excellent place-names index to assist the researcher in locating the jurisdiction under which each town is filed. This is especially useful in finding the correct jurisdictions for German places before 1918. For example:

Essens, Germany converts to: Germany, Preussen, Hanover, Friesland, Essens; and Armentères, France to: France, Nord, Armentères.

The Family History Library has produced numerous excellent research papers for countries of major genealogical interest, including the Netherlands. A complete list of these Dutch papers and their microfiche numbers is appended to chapter 3. Parts of these papers are now out of date and the library will not reprint them. However, as long as they last, copies may be purchased for a nominal fee at the family history centers or by writing the Correspondence Unit, Family History Library, 35 North West Temple Street, Salt Lake City, Utah 84150.

When paper copies are no longer available, the researcher may order them on microfiche from a local family history center, to be used there indefinitely by all patrons. Many updated and additional papers will eventually become available.

The series of Netherlands research papers form a guide to using the Family History Library's Netherlands collection. The first paper in the series, *Major Genealogical Record Sources in the Netherlands*, summarizes what is available:

Major sources are listed with type of record, period covered, type of information included and source availability. Table A shows at a glance the record sources available for a research problem in a particular century. Table B provides more detailed information about the major records available.[5]

There is a separate paper for each province of the Netherlands, listing all the towns and their church records. Once the correct jurisdiction has been ascertained for the ancestor's town of origin, it is then possible to use the paper dealing with the records in the particular province in greater detail. The format followed in these individual papers is basically the same as for the first, but on a different level.

This series also includes a separate paper on each of the main religions, e.g., the Dutch Reformed, Walloon or French Reformed, Evangelical Lutheran, Restored Evangelical Lutheran, Remonstrant, Mennonite, and Roman Catholic.

There are also three other invaluable papers, *Church and Civil Records of Amsterdam, the Netherlands, before 1811* (as already discussed in chapter 2); *The Origins of Names and Their Effect on Genealogical Research in the Netherlands*; and *Historical Background Affecting Genealogical Research in the Netherlands*. A complete list is to follow.

Regardless of the country researched, the same procedure should be followed using applicable guides to assure the greatest success possible. German, French, and Belgian research aids, which are relevant to researching New Netherland settlers, will be discussed later.

Histories

The part history plays in the study of genealogy is well expressed in the introductory remarks of the Family History Library's *Historical Background Affecting Genealogical Research in the Netherlands*:

---

[5] *Major Genealogical Record Sources in the Netherlands*; FHL C: 3, MF 6000039, p. 1.

Successful research in genealogy requires knowledge not only of the types of records available, but also some knowledge of historical background. Genealogy is the study of individuals belonging to the same families; and by its very nature it is related to the history, the time period, and the geographical areas in which those families resided. History itself includes social, economic, political, and religious events as they affected the lives of people.[6]

Since Dutch history with all of its ramifications cannot be covered adequately in this work, reference will be made to sources to which the reader may turn for self-study at various levels of interest. The simplest source is a good chronology of historical events, of which there are many. Some are general, covering the entire history of the Netherlands, e.g. *The Netherlands: A Chronology and Fact Book, 57 B.C.-1971.*[7] Others are limited to one field of interest; for example, the one by George B. Fisher in *The Reformation.*[8] This work examines the various religious factors influencing the migration of people through the Netherlands during the seventeenth century. From the standpoint of meeting the needs of the genealogist, the pamphlet on Netherlands history published by the Family History Library, as before referenced,[9] contains the best chronology in this author's opinion.

If one desires a more detailed study of the Netherlands' historical background in the seventeenth century, the author recommends one of the very few books written in English,

---

[6] *Historical Background Affecting Genealogical Research in the Netherlands*; FHL C: 32.

[7] Pamela Smit and J. W. Smit, comps. and eds., *The Netherlands: A Chronology and Fact Book, 57 B.C. - 1971* (Dobbs Ferry, N.Y.: Oceana Publishers, 1973); not in FHL.

[8] George B. Fisher, *The Reformation* (New York: Charles Scribner's Sons, 1886); not in FHL.

[9] *Historical Background*; FHL C: 32, pp. 9-19.

Peter Geyl's *The Netherlands in the Seventeenth Century.*[10]
The Family History Library does not have this work; however, it may be possible to obtain it at a local library or on
inter-library loan. The maps alone are well worth the effort
to obtain the book.

On the other hand, the Family History Library does have
the well-recognized work by John Lothrop Motley, *History of
the United Netherlands.* ... [11] Unfortunately, it is not on film
for use at the family history centers. But the reader may
follow the same procedure as mentioned above to obtain this
work. It covers the period of Dutch history prior to 1609,
when Spain, exhausted by its wars of conquest, was com-
pelled to sign a twelve-year truce with the Netherlands in
order to regroup. This book provides much background
material to better interpret events which followed.

Certainly some type of historical study should be undertaken to gain a better knowledge of the circumstances
affecting one's ancestors and to put "meat on the bones," so
to speak. Bringing them to life as real human beings makes
their story much more exciting. Knowing their part in the
chain of world events helps those of the present generation
fit themselves into the great "fabric of history."

Patronymics, Surnames, and the Dutch Naming System

In order to find an early ancestor in the Netherlands, not
only is it necessary to pinpoint the exact location to begin researching, it is also imperative to ascertain the many name
variations under which he or she may be found. Overlooking

---

[10] Pieter Geyl, *The Netherlands in the Seventeenth Century*, 2 vols.
(London: Ernest Benn, 1961); not in FHL.

[11] John Lothrop Motley, *History of the United Netherlands.* . . , 4 vols.
(New York: Harper & Bros., 1870); FHL 1181861, its. 1-4.

or misinterpreting just one of these may lead the researcher down the wrong path, resulting in a completely erroneous pedigree. The study of patronymics and the Dutch naming system is a science in itself. With a little practice, a workable knowledge of the subject may be obtained by any studious researcher. However, lacking a fluency in Dutch may limit the person to several works in English and a few simple name books in Dutch.

To begin with, the researcher is referred to a concise treatment of the subject by Rosalie Fellows Bailey, "Dutch Systems in Family Naming: New York and New Jersey,"[12] and two comprehensive pamphlets put out by the Family History Library, *The Origins of Names and Their Effect on Genealogical Research in the Netherlands*,[13] and an address by the late Kenn Stryker-Rodda, *New Netherland Naming Systems and Customs*.[14]

During the Dutch occupation of New Netherland and for some time thereafter, the Dutch generally continued to use the patronymic, which simply means, as Webster says, "a name derived from that of the father or a paternal ancestor, usually by the addition of an affix." In other words, using the father's given name, e.g. Jan, + s, z, sz, se, sen, szen, meaning "son of Jan or Jan's son," as the last name of his son; and Jan(+)s, short for "dochter," for his daughters. All

---

[12] Rosalie Fellows Bailey, "Dutch Systems in Family Naming: New York and New Jersey," *National Genealogical Society Quarterly*, 47 (March 1953): 1-11; (December 1953) 109-18; reprinted as National Genealogical Society Special Publication No. 12, 1965.

[13] *The Origins of Names and Their Effects on Genealogical Research in the Netherlands*; FHL C: 28, MF 6000059.

[14] Kenn Stryker-Rodda, "New Netherland Naming Systems and Customs," *World Conference on Records and Genealogical Seminar, Salt Lake City, Utah, U.S.A., 5-8 August 1969*, Area 1-27 (Salt Lake City: The Church of Jesus Christ of Latter-day Saints, 1969); FHL 0897217, it. 25, MF 6039411.

children of Jan Barents (Jan son of Barent) would be named Jans, for example, Barent Jansz and Debra Jans (children of Jan).

A form of the mother's name (matronym) could also be used; it will not be discussed here, as it was not nearly as prevalent and was virtually unknown in New Netherland. As long as the Dutch remained an agrarian society living in small villages, people generally knew all their neighbors, and the simple patronymic system satisfied the need to distinguish themselves. However, as the population grew and developed large cities, the number of given names remained fairly static. The result was a large number of totally unrelated persons bearing the same combination of names.

The easiest way out of the resulting confusion was for all members of the same family to adopt the current patronymic as the "hereditary surname," sometimes referred to as a "frozen" patronymic, to be used by their descendants throughout future generations. Thus Pieter Jansen's children became Jansen, not Pietersen, etc.

Other permanent Dutch surnames were adopted from the locality where some member of the family once lived or from the name of his farm, for example Van der Meide (from the field), Van Borsum (a town), Van Zwolle, Van Antwerp, Van Rensselaer.

At times a "trade-name" was added like de Clerq (the clerk), de Kuijper (the cooper), de Potter (the potter); or a personal characteristic such as de Bruijn (the bear), Swart (dark complected). A good book on the origin and meaning of Dutch and Flemish given names is *Het namenboek*.[15]

A man may have been known at different times by any one or combination of the above, even by different names in the same record source, not to mention variations of spelling. A case in point is Jacob Swart who was known in his marriage intention and the baptisms of his four children in

---

[15] A. N. W. van der Plank, *Het namenboek* (Bussum: Unieboek bv., 1979); n.m.

Amsterdam as Jacob Ilkers, Jacob Hilkersz, Jacob Willemsz Hilkers, Jacob Willemsz, and Jacob Hellers. Quoting from the author's article "Jacob Hellekers Alias Swart and Some of His Descendants":

> Since the patronymic 'Willemsz' (son of Willem) was given in the second baptismal entry, and Jacob named his son Willem, it is evident his father's given name was Willem. However, a question arises concerning his second patronymic or surname. He signed his marriage intention, an official document written in Dutch, as Jacob 'Ilkers,' probably the patronymic form of the given name Ilke (r).[16]
>
> The use of two patronymics, Willemsz and Ilkers, suggests Jacob's mother may have married twice, the first husband named Willem and the second Ile(r). It is also possible Jacob took his grandfather's given name, as was the custom if the grandfather were a man of means or influence (conversation in 1974 with Hendrick O. Slok). Of course, the chance exists that Ilkers had become a 'set surname' in the area where he was born.
>
> In New Netherland Jacob never used the form Ilkers or the patronymic Willemez. By that time Ilkers had evolved to Hellekers, and he also became known as the 'black carpenter' and then as 'Swart' [swarthy complected].[17]

Another interesting case of multiple names for one man is given in Bailey's article:

> The emigrant ancestor of the Quick family of New York and New Jersey appears on different records with four different 'last' names: his patronymic, his surname, his place of origin, and his trade. That they belong to one man is proved by the appearance of his wife Belitje Jacobs in conjunction with them. On 1645-1659 court and land records covering one lot, he is Teunis Tomassen Van Naarden and also Teunis Tomassen Quick. On the first and third baptismal entries for their children in New Amsterdam given below, his name on the printed version appears as Theunis Thomas; Theunis Thomasz, Metselaer [the butcher]; Teunis Thomaszen Met-

---

[16] A. Huizinga, *Encyclopedie van voornamen* (Amsterdam: A.J.G. Strengholt's, 1957), p. 123; n.m.

[17] Gwenn F. Epperson, "Jacob Hellekers Alias Swart and Some of His Descendants," REC. 121 (1990): 14.

selaer; Theunis Thomas, Metselaer; and Theunis de Metselaer; but on the original records, is shown as Theunis Thomas; Theunis Thomas metselaer; Teunis Thomaszen metselaer; Theunis Thomas, metselaer; and Theunis de metselaer.[18]

Bailey gives other enlightening information concerning this name. Further study of her article is recommended. The establishment of surnames came about in a very haphazard manner over a long period of time. Among descendants of New Netherland settlers in the late seventeenth and early eighteenth centuries, use of the patronymic system declined. Various members of the same family often adopted different surnames. An example is the case of the family of "Jan Evertsen, Master Shoemaker of Albany" (as previously referenced) who came on 19 May 1658 in *The Gilded Beaver*. His only surviving son Evert took his father's given name as his patronymic and became Evert Janse or Jansen. He had three sons, Jan, Jacob, and Hanns. All three took their father's given name "Evert" as their patronymic according to custom and went by Evertse or Evertsen. However, in the next or fourth generation the children of John [Jan] and Hanns were known as "Janse or Jansen" while those of Jacob became "Evertse or Evertsen." These names were "set" or "frozen" patronymics by which their families were known throughout succeeding generations. The many changes created much confusion for ministers and genealogists alike.

The same process was going on in the old country. Quoting from the very informative research paper developed by the Family History Library entitled *The Origins of Names*:

> By decree of the Emperor Napoleon in 1811, all Netherlands families were required to have fixed surnames, but many Dutch surnames developed much earlier, even as early as the sixteenth and seventeenth centuries. When a family adopted a surname depended on the area of residence, social status, and other factors. The general pattern of surname development in the Netherlands was

---

[18] Bailey, "Family Naming," NGSQ 47: 9.

from south to north.
The nobility were the first to adopt family names from the names of the estates where they originally resided. . . .[19]

In his talk at the World Conference on Records, Stryker-Rodda gives his theory concerning the end of patronymics in New Netherland:

> The English, therefore, insisted upon members of the same family using the "same last name." The first official list extant, the oath list for Kings County, made in September 1687, shows that the crusade was not uniformly successful.[20]

The question may well be asked, how can genealogical research be performed, considering the confusion surrounding the use of Dutch surnames? There are several suggestions which, if followed, will insure the best results.

During the seventeenth century a Dutch woman retained her maiden name after marriage, and it generally did not undergo many changes like the husband's. So once the name of the wife is ascertained, this is one tool for locating the records, especially if it is a set surname or the name is fairly unusual. To obtain any possible baptisms of children, it is well to search church records for at least twenty-five years from the date of marriage, under first the husband's name and then the wife's.

The second convenient tool is comparing the given names of children with those of witnesses or sponsors in Dutch Church baptisms in America as well as the Netherlands. Well into the eighteenth century, the Dutch had close relatives stand as sponsors at the baptisms of children. These relatives are additional leads for research.

The two eldest sons and two eldest daughters were generally named after the four grandparents. In naming

---

[19] *The Origins of Names*; FHL C: 28, MF 6000059, p. 8.

[20] Kenn Stryker-Rodda, *New Netherland Naming Systems and Customs*, Area 1-27: 4.

these children an exception to the grandparent rule was often made to honor a close relative who had recently died. Then the rest were usually named after the parents, great-grandparents, uncles and aunts, often alternating names from each side of the family. If a child died young, the next child of the same sex was usually named for the deceased child, sometimes up to three or more in the same family.

If the husband or wife died and there were a second marriage, often the first child by that marriage was named after the deceased spouse or a child by the first marriage.

A good example using these principles is the Rutgers family included in the article by Bailey. The only deviation is that the group of children by the second wife did not contain enough boys to name one after her father. As the author states, the example is "far more perfect than will usually be found." There were two marriages for the father. Anthony Rutgers, son of Harmanus Rutgers and Catarine Hooges, married first 1698, Hendrickje van de Water, daughter of Pieter van de Water and Annetje Duycking:

Children

i.	Harmanus d.y.	Anthony's father
ii.	Petrus	Hendrickje's father
iii.	Catharyna d.y.	Anthony's mother
iv.	Anneke	Hendrickje's mother
v.	Catharina d.y. (repeat)	Anthony's mother
vi.	Anthony d.y.	Anthony's grandfather
vii.	Catharina (repeat)	Anthony's mother
viii.	Anthony d.y. (repeat)	Anthony's grandfather
ix.	Maria d.y.	Hendrickje's great aunt

Anthony Rutgers married second 1716, Cornelia (Roos) Benson, widow, daughter of Johannes Roos and Cornelia:

Children

i. Anthony (twin)	Anthony's grandfather
(repeat)	
ii. Harmanus d.y.	Anthony's father
iii. Cornelia d.y.	Cornelia and mother
iv. Elsje	Anthony's aunt
v. Maria	" "
(repeat)	
vi. Aletta	" " [21]

Of course, there were some "variations on theme" when naming Dutch children. A number of families followed these practices rigidly while others modified the system to their liking. But some form of this system was generally used. A good example of naming variations is provided by the family of Egbert van Borsum and Annetje Hendricks in the author's article on this family. The Van Borsum family was fairly easy to follow in Amsterdam, as they were using set surnames made from the name of a town (Borsum) in the area of Niedersachsen Land (Lower Saxony State), in northwestern Germany.[22]

However, Egbert's wife Annetje Hendricks was born in Amsterdam and was known only by her patronymic. A search of baptismal records disclosed an entry in the Nieuwekerk (New Church) which reads:

6 August 1619 was baptized Annetje daughter of Henrick Hermansz and Griet Centen, witness: Beltje Groessens.[23]

Two marriages were found for this Henrick Hermansz, to Jannetjen Tijmans and Griet Centens. He had one child, Herman, by the first marriage, and seven by the second, all

---

[21] Bailey, "Family Naming," NGSQ 47: 113.

[22] REC. 119 (1988): 85-89.

[23] Ibid., p. 88.

baptized in the Nieuwekerk and Oudekerk.[24]
To quote the Van Borsum article:

> The question now arises, has the correct line been followed for
> Annetje Hendricks' ancestry? A comparison of the given names of
> her children (in order of baptism) with names in Egbert van Bor-
> sum's family and in her "supposed" line produces good evidence in
> support of that line:

> i. Hermanus - Annetje's brother and paternal grandfather.
> ii. Cornelis - Egbert's brother.
> iii. Barent - Egbert's brother.
> iv. Hendrick - Annetje's father.
> v. Tijmon - Annetje's step-grandfather.
> vi. Janneken - Annetje's step-mother.
> vii. Annetje - Annetje's deceased sister and herself.[25]

A small book the author relies on to interpret archaic
Dutch given names, *Woordenboek van voornamen* (a dictionary of given names), was consulted concerning the patronymic Centens.[26] The Van Borsum article explains:

> The surname Senten or Centen is really a patronymic made
> from the male given name "Sent," or Vincent. The female form is
> found as Senta, Senske, Sente, Sentiene, or Sentsje. In the 17th
> century, these names were used frequently in the province of
> Friesland, the birthplace of Griet Senten.[27]

There are two other good sources on the subject of Dutch

---

[24] Ibid., pp. 88-89.

[25] Ibid., p. 89.

[26] Johannes van der Schaar, *Woordenboek van voornamen*, 5th ed.
(Utrecht: Uitgeverij het Spectrum, 1970); n.m.

[27] REC. 119 (1988): 89.

given names; *Onze voornamen* (our given names)[28] by J.A. Meijers, and J.C. Luitingh and A. Huizinga's *Encyclopedia van voornamen* (encyclopedia of given names), previously referenced. The latter book covers the origins and meanings of Dutch and Flemish given names.

A suggestion for distinguishing between men with the same given name and patronymic is to obtain the trade of each. This method of identification was used successfully in the case of Evert Janse or Jansen, son of Jan Evertsen, for the article already referenced, to separate the records of Evert Jansen, cooper, from those of Evert Jansen Wendel, tailor, both with wives Maria, and living in Albany during the same time period. The following statement appears in the published Albany Court records:

> As early as 5 December 1676 in an Ordinary Court Session held in Albany, Evert Jansen was known also as "Evert de Cuyper" (cooper), as were his sons, after their trade. However, there is no evidence "Cooper" was added to the [patronymic or] surname as in many other cases. . . .

A footnote to the above session says:

> 'This man is Evert Jansen, cooper. He has by [Jonathan] Pearson been confused with Evert Jansen Wendel who was a tailor by trade.[29]

Of course, if the researcher is fortunate enough to find the signature or mark of the man in question, this almost may be proof positive of his identity. However, the author has found even some signatures change over the years.

During the seventeenth century and even earlier it was

---

[28] J.A. Meijers and J.C. Luitingh, *Onze voornamen* (Amsterdam: Moussault's Uitgeverij, 1966); n.m.

[29] Arnold J.F. van Laer, trans. and ed., *Minutes of the Court of Albany, Rensselaerswyck, and Schenectady, 1668-1685*, 3 vols. (Albany: University of the State of New York, 1926-1932); MF 6087906-8.

popular in the Netherlands to use a special mark on the house door to identify the family living there. These symbols were known as "huismerken" (house marks) and were sometimes used with or without the signature on official documents. Examples of over 2000 of these marks can be found in L. F. van Gent's *Een wereldreis van 2000 huismerken, met 2170 teekeningen*.[30] They were gathered in the town of Nijmegen but are characteristic of those found throughout the Netherlands. The book includes a short history of the signs. The earliest "huismerk" mentioned dates back to 1520. The signs began with a few simple lines, which were added to when the person married or joined a guild. Eventually "huismarken" became like modern monograms or crests and were identifying marks.

Dictionaries, Handwriting, and Word Lists

Since reading seventeenth-century Dutch records poses the greatest challenge to those searching for New Netherland ancestors, several aids will be required to complete the task with any degree of accuracy.

The first research tool in this group is an old Dutch-English dictionary, of which there are many at the Family History Library. The author has found them useful in determining the meanings of obsolete terms not found in modern Dutch-English dictionaries. As stated before, the one the author prefers, which is also found on microfilm to be used at the family history centers, is the one by Van Goor.[31]

---

[30] L.F. van Gent, *Een wereldreis van 2000 huismarken, met 2170 tee-keningen* (Arnhem: S. Gouda Quint-D. Brouwer en Zoon, 1944); n.m.

[31] *Van Goor Dictionary.*

The main records likely to be used in early Dutch research are church registers. Fortunately, a standardized format is used, only changing occasionally when a new minister takes over. Therefore, if one entry is difficult to read, it is only necessary to look for another more legible one to see much of the same wording. The same suggestion applies for reading given names and patronymics. Likewise individual letters can often be deciphered by finding them in another recognizable word. This method is also followed by the most knowledgeable researchers.

There are many word lists available, including an excellent one published by the Family History Library entitled *Genealogical Word List: Dutch*, and available at a nominal cost.[32] It includes a large number of words found in Dutch records with their English translations, and also the numbers, months, days of the week, and times of the day in Dutch.

According to Slok, there are several notable differences between English and Dutch alphabetizing of indexes:

> All names in the indexes are arranged alphabetically without regard to prefixes. The exact treatment depends on the index and the time period. . . .

In other words, the Dutch would normally index Van Borsum under Borsum, or De Planck under Planck, while in an American index they would be found under V and D.

Slok continues:

> Following is a list of some modern letter (sound) combinations with their old equivalent spellings that appear in the index:

---

[32] *Genealogical Word List: Dutch*, Family History Library pamphlet.

Modern	Old Spelling	Modern	Old Spelling
a	aa	o	oe
aa	ae	oe	oi oo oij oy
ak	ac ack	oo	oeoi
au	ou	ou	au
c	ck k x cx	q	kw
ek	eck	s	ss sz z x
f	ff ph	u	v
g	ch gh	ui	ue uij vy w
i	j ij y	v	u
ie	je ije ye y	w	uu ui uij uy vv
j	i ij y	vij	ie eij iij
k	c	x	ks s cs
ks	cx	z	s sz ss
kw	q		

Even the best dictionary will be of no value if the researcher cannot decipher the handwriting. Seventeenth-century Dutch documents are usually written in a script very different from our own. Attention is called to two excellent little books on Dutch handwriting by Hans Brouwer, former Chief Archivist at the Rijksarchief in The Hague. Although written in Dutch, nevertheless the illustrations will be helpful to anyone doing seventeenth-century Dutch research.

The first is *Beknopte handleiding tot de kennis van het Nederlandsche oude schrift* (condensed guide to old Dutch writing).[33] The second is a revised version of the first, *Geschreven Verleden: genealogie en oud schrift* (genealogy and old handwriting).[34] These books contain an alphabet with both upper- and lower-case letters in seventeenth-century Dutch handwriting and a rather comprehensive word list required for genealogical research in both the old handwriting and

---

[33] Hans Brouwer, *Beknopte handleiding tot de kennis van het Nederlandsche oude schrift* (Naarden: N. V. Uitgevers and Maatschappij A. Rutgers, 1941); FHL 0198725.

[34] Hans Brouwer, *Geschreven Verleden: genealogie en oud schrift* (s'Gravenhage: Europese Bibliotheek, 1963); n.m.

print. They also contain a number of handwritten documents with printed copies included, taken from old civil records and parish registers.

An even more thorough study of Dutch handwriting is found in the textbook for a two-year homestudy course on Flemish paleography, *Oud schrift: kursus per briefwisseling*,[35] in three volumes. The course was developed in Belgium, and therefore is written in Flemish, one of the official languages of that country. Flemish and Dutch are essentially the same language, despite differences in their written forms. The books are replete with illustrations of various forms of each letter of the alphabet, plus other research aids.

In conclusion, not only is it necessary to find the Dutch records required for ancestral research, it is also vital to read them correctly. With dictionaries, Dutch word lists, and guides to old handwriting, the necessary acumen can be acquired in a reasonably short period of time. As the old adage says, "Practice makes perfect!"

---

[35]   Centrum voor Familiegeschiedenis, *Oud schrift: kursus per briefwisseling*, 3 vols., (Antwerp: n.p., 1968); n.m.

GENEALOGICAL RESEARCH PAPERS

FOR

THE NETHERLANDS

by the Family History Library

The research papers covering the Netherlands are listed under "Series C." The individual numbers within the series, the titles, and microfiche numbers follow:

3. *Major Genealogical Record Sources in the Netherlands*; MF 6000039.

5. *Guide to Genealogical Sources in the Netherlands--Zeeland*; MF 6000041.

6. *Guide to Genealogical Sources in the Netherlands--Groningen*; MF 6000042.

7. *Guide to Genealogical Sources in the Netherlands--Friesland*; MF 6000043.

8. *Guide to Genealogical Sources in the Netherlands--Overijssel*; MF 6000044.

9. *Guide to Genealogical Sources in the Netherlands--Gelderland*; MF 6000045.

10. *Guide to Genealogical Sources in the Netherlands--North Holland*; MF 6000046.

11. *Guide to Genealogical Sources in the Netherlands--Utrecht*; MF 6000047.

12. *Guide to Genealogical Sources in the Netherlands--Limburg*; MF 6000048.

13. *Guide to Genealogical Sources in the Netherlands--North Brabant*; MF 6000049.

14. *Guide to Genealogical Sources in the Netherlands--South Holland*; MF 6000050.

15. *Guide to Genealogical Sources in the Netherlands--Drenthe*; MF 6000051.

20. *Church Records of the Netherlands--Remonstrant Church*; MF 6000052.

21. *Church Records of the Netherlands--Mennonites*; MF 6000053.

22. *Church Records of the Netherlands--Dutch Reformed*; MF 6000054.

23. *Church Records of the Netherlands--Walloon or French Reformed*; MF 6000055.

24. *Church Records of the Netherlands--Evangelical Lutheran and Restored Evangelical Lutheran*; MF 6000056.

25. *Church and Civil Records of Amsterdam, the Netherlands, before 1811*; MF 6000355-6000356.

26. *Church Records of the Netherlands--Roman Catholic*; MF 6000058.

28. *The Origins of Names and Their Effect on Genealogical Research in the Netherlands*; MF 6000059.

32. *Historical Background Affecting Genealogical Research in the Netherlands*: n. MF.

4 FINDING AND SEARCHING EUROPEAN PARISH REGISTERS

The Netherlands

As for other European countries, there are many civil records and secondary sources for the Netherlands. However, without a working knowledge of the Dutch language, the researcher is almost entirely limited to using parish registers for obtaining genealogical information. Armed with the Dutch ancestor's place of origin and necessary "research aids," the researcher is now prepared to locate and use the appropriate parish registers.

To establish which registers are available for the applicable time period, the best and most convenient starting point is Slok's guide to genealogical sources[1] followed by the separate guide for each province listed at the end of chapter 3. These guides follow essentially the same format. They contain many useful aids including a list of historical data affecting the province, and a map of the Netherlands after 1648, when the country gained its independence following the eighty-years war with Spain.

However, the most important section, which occupies the larger portion of each guide, contains a map of the province divided into municipalities; a place-name key to the towns and their appropriate municipalities; and a chart listing the towns under their municipalities. Among the various sources listed in the chart are Dutch Reformed, Roman Catholic, and other church records with their years of availability. Having determined that the church registers exist, it is then only necessary to consult the Family History Library Catalog

---

[1] *Major Genealogical Record Sources in the Netherlands*; FHL C: 3, MF 6000039.

for the microfilm numbers of these records.

The researcher will possibly come across the *Repertorium DTB* (published index of all Dutch parish registers of baptisms, marriages, and burials, prior to civil registration),[2] and similar indexes for each individual province of the Netherlands. They are an alternative to the Slok papers, although they do not contain any research aids and are written entirely in Dutch. *After* they were microfilmed some thoughtful person wrote the film call numbers in the books, but unfortunately, the researcher must use them in the main library in Salt Lake City to benefit from this addition.

Van Barkello Family

An ideal example of using church registers to trace a family back to the Netherlands is provided by Slok's article in the *Record*, "The Dutch Ancestry of the Van Barkello Family in Early Kings County New York: in the Netherlands."[6]

By using the passenger lists it was determined that "Willem Jansz, from Berckeloo and Harman Jansen, from Berckeloo, wife and two children, 5, and 3 years old" came in *De Trouw (The Faith)* on 24 March 1662.[4] They are also listed in Bailey's article in the *Record*, regarding the account book of the Dutch West India Company, which adds the information that both men were farmers.[5]

---

[2] William Wijnaendts van Resandt, *Repertorium DTB*, ed. and comp. J.G.J. van Booma [Den Haag]: Centraal bureau voor Genealogie, 1969; FHL 0908159, it. 1.

[3] Hendrik O. Slok, "The Dutch Ancestry of the Van Barkello Family in Early Kings County New York: in the Netherlands," REC. 115 (1984): 193-98, reprinted as Appendix A in this guide.

[4] HSYB 1902: 19; FHL 098989, it. 5.

[5] REC. 94 (1963): 196.

A footnote to Bailey's article states:

'William Jansz van borkello,' as he signed his name, had first come
here by 1658 when he married. On the 1662 trip he brought his
brother (next in the account book), and from them descend the
Van Barkelo family.[6]

Quoting again from Slok's article:

The name of Harman's wife can be found in the joint will [with]
her second husband, Hans Harmansz;[7] she is referred to as
Willemtjen Warnaers also surnamed Eldringh elsewhere in the
records. In this document her children by Harmen Jansz, her first
husband, named Jannetje, Reynier, Harman, . . . were to receive a
legacy. In the will dated 12 November 1694, Willemptje's patronymic is Warnaers. The first two children mentioned in the ships
listing are Jannetje and Reynier, born respectively about 1657 and
1659 in the Netherlands.

All the before mentioned information formed the basis for
research in the Borculo [present spelling] area records in the
province of Gelderland, the Netherlands.[8]

Van der Aa's gazetteer produced a reference to the town
of Borkelo:

Borkelo of Borkeloe, oude naam van het platteland stadje Borculo,
in het graafschaap Zutphen, prov. Gelderland.

Borkelo or Borkeloe, old name of the small country town Borculo,
in the county of Sutphen, province of Gelderland.[9]

---

[6] Ibid., 200.

[7] Calendar of New Jersey Wills, 1670-1817, Archives of the State of New
Jersey, First Series, vols. 23, 30, 32-42 (Trenton, New Jersey: 1901-49), 21:
145.

[8] REC. 115 (1984): 194.

[9] Van der Aa, Aardrijkskundig woordenboek, 2: 596.

A review of Slok's guide listing the extant records of the province Gelderland reveals the following Dutch Reformed Church records for the town of Borculo under the municipality by the same name:

> *Borculo*: Christenings 1616-
> Marriages 1616-31, 1666-1810
> Deaths 1665-[10]

Slok goes on to say:

> Searches in the Borculo DRC records 1653-1663 failed to disclose any information concerning Willem or Harmen Jansz and wife. The expression "van (from) Borculo" could also refer to the Jurisdiction--Court Jurisdiction of Borculo which contains the villages and hamlets, some with their own churches, of Geesteren, Geeselaer, and Haarlo.[11]

Slok's guide discloses the following reference to extant Dutch Reformed Church Records in Geesteren:

> *Geesteren*: Christenings, marriages, and members 1651-; Deaths 1742-1798.[12]

A search in the Geesteren Dutch Reformed Church records produced the following interesting entry (See Illustration 2):

> Membership records, list made up in 1655: *Harmen* Lubberdinck & vrou, added later, *verreist nae nieu Nederlandt* [*Harman* Lubberdinck

---

[10] *Guide to Genealogical Sources in the Netherlands--Gelderland*; FHL C: 9, MF 6000045, p. 12.

[11] REC. 115 (1984): 195.

[12] *Guide to Sources in Gelderland*, p. 14.

& wife, traveled to new Netherland.][13]

Slok's research illustrates a very important point. The ancestor may not always be found in the place of origin given in New Netherland records. In some cases when it was a tiny, obscure village or the family left records in several small villages, the name of the larger municipality was given for better identification. In this situation an area search in all existing church records for each hamlet within the municipality will be necessary to identify every member of the family. Explaining the surnames used in this family, Slok calls attention to another aspect often overlooked by researchers. He says:

> Lubbeerdinck, a farmstead on which they [the Van Barkeloo family] resided for several generations, is located southeast of Geesteren. In America, this very local name was superseded by *van Barculoo*.[14]

Additional information on the use of farm names as surnames is supplied by C. Roodenburg, a Dutch genealogist of Haarlem:

> Many surnames were derived from the names of farms on which our forefathers lived and whose descendants still live there now. Especially in the Eastern part of the Netherlands a man was named for the name of his farmstead. With many farmer families these names finally became surnames and were enforced by Napoleonic Laws. When moving to another farm, the name of the new farm was adopted.
>
> If there were several sons in a farmer family it often happened that the eldest son (sometimes the youngest) would settle on the parental farmstead and the other sons received new farms or a farm would be bought for them; they then received the name of that farm as the surname. It is therefore possible that persons with

---

[13] REC. 115 (1984): 195; Membership Records DRC of Geesteren, 336: n.p.; FHL 0108713.

[14] REC. 115 (1984): 195.

different surnames can have the same progenitor. Before 1812 there were no surnames enforced by law and everyone was free to change his surname.[15]

A marriage entry for Harmen Lubberdinck alias Van Barkeloo and his wife Willemken Warners Elderinck was also found in the Geesteren records:

27 March 1653:
Harmen Lubberdinck son of Jan Lubberdinck from Geesteren
with
Willemken Elderinck daughter of Warner Elderinck from Hengelo
and married there 11 April.[16]

The baptisms of three children for this couple were found. In the baptismal records of Hengelo, another municipality, the entry of the firstborn child was registered: "27 March 1654, Herman Lubberdinck of Elderinck held his own daughter Janneken when she was baptized. Witnesses Henrica Waerle, Henrick te Holte's daughter Heijntie, and his wife's sister."[17] This child must have died soon after baptism, as the name was repeated again for the next child.

The other two children were baptized in the records of the church at Geesteren as translated:

27 April 1656: Harmen Lubberdinck's and Willemken's daughter Jenneke baptized. Witnesses: Warner Elderinck, Geesken Lubberdinck & Otjen Mols.

---

[15] C. Roodenburg, "Genealogical Research Problems in the Netherlands," *World Conference on Records and Genealogical Seminar*, Salt Lake City, Utah, U.S.A. 5-8 August, 1969. Area D5 & 6e (Salt Lake City: The Church of Jesus Christ of Latter-day Saints, 1969); FHL 0897214, it. 29, MF 6039326.

[16] REC. 115 (1984): 195; Marriages DRC of Geesteren, 336: n.p.; FHL 0108713.

[17] REC. 115 (1984): 195; Baptisms DRC of Hengelo, 910: n.p.; FHL 0108743.

5 Jume 1659: Harmen Lubberdinck's and Willemken's son Reint baptized. Witnesses: the Noble squire Reiner van Duithe named Buth toe Mensinck, Jan Lubberdinck the Elder and Griete Mols.[18]

Slok concludes:

When these entries are compared with what is known from American sources, little doubt is left as to the identity of these individuals: Harmen Jansz Lubberdinck and wife Willemken Warners Elderinck and children Jenneke (Jannetje) and Reint (Reynier) ages 5 and 3 years, traveled to New Netherland after 1655.[19]

Using church and civil records for villages within the Court Jurisdictions of Borculo, Hengelo, and Lochem, Slok was able to identify relatives back several generations. A study of this article will benefit even the most competent researcher.

Regardless of the area in the Netherlands from which the researcher's family came, the research can follow the same general guidelines explained here with very few exceptions. However, many ancestors long thought to be Dutch will prove to be of other nationalities.

Germany

Prior to 1792 when civil registration began in some parts of Germany, parish registers were the only records which provided any type of detailed information on most of the population. Therefore, they form the most important source for German genealogical research. However, due to the unsettled political history of the country, locating the records can be a challenge.

---

[18] REC. 115 (1984): 195; Baptisms DRC of Geesteren, 336: n.p.; FHL 0108713.

[19] REC. 115 (1984): 195.

Understanding the status of religion in sixteenth- and seventeenth-century Germany will be helpful in searching for parish registers. The country was not unified but rather made up of a number of small kingdoms, duchies, and other entities with absolute rulers who determined which religion would be practiced in their areas. Therefore, there was no separation of church and state. In fact, the church and state were one. Since there was only one official religion allowed in each area, the researcher will generally find one church of a single denomination in most small towns.

Until Martin Luther nailed his ninety-five theses on the door of the castle church in Wittenburg on the eve of the Feast of All Saints, 31 October 1517, the churches were uniformly Roman Catholic, and any records kept were in Latin. However, from 1517 on there were religious wars between Catholic and Protestant factions. When the Protestants prevailed, crucifixes and other religious emblems were tossed outside and broken. At times the Catholics returned and restored the churches as before.

Even the Protestants were not unified:

> Protestant Germany was not an underlying unity with differences of opinion. . . . In divided Germany Lutherans would not allow either the mass or the Calvinist [Reformed] worship in Lutheran states; the Calvinist consistories would discipline anyone found holding Catholic or Lutheran doctrines of the Real Presence. Because there were more separated Protestant states in Germany than elsewhere, the religious disunity of Germany was more manifest.[20]

Most areas eventually accepted one faith or another and remain so today, generally Protestant in the North and Catholic in the South.

Turning to the history of parish registers and their contents, some church records were kept in Germany as early as

---

[20] Owen Chadwick, ed., *The Reformation*, vol. 3 of *The Pelican History of the Church* (Harmondsworth, Eng.: Penguin Books, 1964. Reprint. 1975), p. 151; not at FHL.

the fifteenth century but very few pre-Reformation church records have survived. Beginning with the Reformation the earliest extant parish registers are Protestant. Quoting from a very detailed paper by the Family History Library (on microfiche) entitled *The Church Records of Germany*:

> Few Roman Catholic Church registers have survived from the period prior to the Thirty Years' War (1618-1648), even though the Catholics were commanded to keep records from the time of the Council of Trent in 1563. It was not until after the Thirty Years' War, however, that record keeping became general practice in all German churches.[21]

Considering the wars, insects, and natural catastrophes, the wonder is, not so much how many parish registers are missing, but how any survived the ravages of time!

The parish registers fall into two categories. The first is those of the ministerial acts as they occurred, primarily baptisms (*Taufen*), marriages (*Heiraten*), and burials (*Begrabnissen*). They may be found in separate volumes or combined in single books recorded together as they occurred. The latter form is particularly common in smaller parishes. The other category is the family registers (*Familien-registers*). They are a great help to the researcher and should be searched whenever they are available. A very fine handout by the Family History Library, but no longer available, entitled *German Primary Sources*, has this to say:

> Family registers are records of complete families, listing the parents and all of their children together. This eliminates searching year after year in the christening [baptism], marriage, and death registers, since all of these dates are given for all individuals that are listed in the family register.

This handout continues:

> There are usually three generations listed on one document in

---

[21] *The Church Records of Germany*; FHL C: 29, p. 2, MF 6000033.

the family register, the father and the mother of the family, all of their children, and the parents of the father and the mother. References where to find additional ancestors, and where to find information on the families of the children who were married are also given. Though family registers are excellent records, they should not be used solely, but should only serve as a guide in finding the original entries. [As with all records the more they are copied the greater risk of error].

In the author's experience information obtained by mail from ministers in Germany is generally taken from the family registers, as the younger clergy are sometimes overworked, underpaid, or unfamiliar with the old script. They do not expect to be paid for their services; however, they are grateful for a small "donation" to their parish. Should individual entries be desired it is usually necessary to hire a researcher or make a visit to the parish in person.

The quality of a German parish register depends largely on the scribe who made the entries. Some clergy took the time to describe events in great detail, even including the prayer which was said, mention of acts of war, and details of plagues and famines. It is not unusual to find facts concerning a death. This concern also shows in the quality of the handwriting which varies vastly among the clergy. The records of more recent years are not always easier to read than those of earlier time periods. In some cases records of the sixteenth century are easier to read than those of the eighteenth or nineteenth.

The parish registers are usually kept in the individual parishes; however, in some areas the oldest ones have been turned over to state or church archives for better preservation.

Having gained an understanding of parish registers and their value, the researcher is faced with the necessity of locating and searching the ancestor's records. German research is greatly simplified by many excellent aids, such as *Meyers Orts- und Verkehrs-lexikon des Deutschen Reichs* (a

gazetteer of Germany before World War I).[22] With this
gazetteer it is possible to locate the town and province,
churches in the town, or the closest church in the area, with
other geographic details. Meyers also gives the former
kingdoms, duchies, etc. to which the towns belonged. This
information is vital to use of the Family History Library
Catalog. All localities are listed in that catalog according to
pre-1918 boundaries.

After ascertaining the pre-1918 jurisdiction it is generally
possible to find the exact location on the map by using the
Konigliche Preussische Landesaufname (maps of the German
Empire, including parts of modern Poland, Russia, Denmark,
Belgium, France, Czechoslovakia, Lithuania, and the
Netherlands 1845-1916).[23] Using a grid system provided at
the beginning of the map, it is possible to find almost any
tiny village in Germany with its surrounding environs. This
feature is especially helpful in performing an area search to
find an ancestor, if this should become necessary.

It is important to know that just because a parish is closer
to the town of origin, it is not necessarily the place where the
ancestor's records can be found. With a change of jurisdiction the registers may have been moved to another parish;
therefore, an area search may become necessary. It is also
advisable to do an area search in surrounding villages with
separate parishes to pick up additional relatives.

Depending on the size and number of inhabitants, larger
towns may have several parishes. Conversely, in some rural
areas of Germany not every small village has its own parish,
and therefore, a number of different villages may belong to
the same parish. Parish record inventories are especially
helpful to the researcher in determining the place to look for

---

[22] E. Uetrecht, comp., *Meyers Orts- und Verkehrs-lexikon des Deutschen
Reichs*, 2 vols. (Leipzig: Bibliographisches Institut, 1912-13); FHL 0496640-
1, MF 6000001-29.

[23] *Konigliche Preussische Landesaufname*, Map. Scale 1:100,000 (Berlin:
Die Landesaufnahme, 1914-17); FHL 0068814.

records of localities that do not have their own parishes. They indicate what records are available and what time periods they cover. Parish register inventories also give historical facts and former names of parishes, as well as information on why certain records are not available. Unfortunately, at this writing no one inventory exists for all parishes in Germany, but they can be found under each province in "Archives and Libraries-Inventories, Catalogs, Registers," in the Family History Library Catalog. An example is *Kirchenbücher und Standesregister für alle wohnplätze im Land Hessen* (an inventory of parish registers and civil records for the former grand duchy of Hessen).[24]

To interpret archaic terms, especially some obsolete occupations found in parish registers, the library has *Hilfwörterbuch für Historiker: Mittelalter und Neuzeit* (a dictionary of German source terminology from the Middle Ages to modern times).[25]

Of course, a list of German words with their English equivalents will be useful, and one can be purchased from the Family History Library and family history centers. An excellent book on German handwriting is Heibert Strum's *Unsere Schrift* (Our Writing).[26] It gives the introduction and development of the Gothic script, handwritten and in print. Another valuable work written for genealogists by Edna M. Bentz is *If I Can, You Can Decipher Germanic Records.*[27] It

---

[24] Otfried Praetorius, *Kirchenbücher und Standesregister für alle Wohnplätze im Land Hessen* (Darmstadt: Selbstverlag der Historischen Kommission für das Land Hessen, 1939); FHL 0492895, MF 6053529.

[25] Eugen Haberkern and Joseph Friedrich Wallach, *Hilfswörterbuch für Historiker: Mittelalter und Neuzeit* (Berne and Munich: Francke Verlag, 1964); n.m.

[26] Heribert Sturm, *Unsere Schrift* (Neustadt on the Aisch and Munich: Degener & Co., 1961); n.m.

[27] Edna M. Bentz, *If I Can, You Can Decipher Germanic Records* (San Diego: E. M. Bentz, 1982); n. m.

includes German terminology written in Gothic script with
English and some Danish and Latin equivalents.

Hardenbrook Family

Referring back to several examples of finding the places
of origin for New Netherland settlers from passenger lists
and marriage records, it was established Adolph Hardenbrook, the immigrant ancestor of the Hardenbrook family,
originated in Elberfeld, Germany. With that knowledge the
Reformed Church parish registers of Elberfeld dating from
1584 were searched with amazing success, resulting in an
article for the *Record* "The European Origin of the Hardenbrook Family."[28]
Although these registers are in extremely bad condition,
and there is a gap in the marriage records from 1620 to
1649, the author was able to put together the family of
Adolph Hardenbrook, or Aloff Hodenbruch (with many
other spelling variations) as he was known in Germany.
"Margreidta," the given name of Adolph's first wife, was
found in a burial record, and the given name of his second,
"Merig or Maria," in two baptisms of their eight children.
However, her full name Maria Caterberg was included in the
membership records of the Dutch Church of New York.[29]
Quoting from the article before referenced:

> The baptisms and marriages covering the proper time period
> were searched several times [for Adolph's parents], keeping in mind
> that Adolph Hardenbrook, in the baptisms of his children, was
> referred to as "Aloff Luckes" as late as 1646. This would indicate
> that he was using a patronymic and his father's given name was
> Lucas. However, the possibility also existed, although not as likely,
> that the patronymic had become a fixed surname and Adolph had
> changed it to "Hoddenbruch" to distinguish it from other families by

---

[28] REC. 117 (1986): 1-7, and Appendix B of this guide.

[29] REC. 9 (1878): 75.

the same surname. Therefore, it was necessary that all entries for men with the given name of "Lucas" be noted.[30]

Only one man by the name of Lucas Barss seemed to be a likely candidate for the father of Aloff Hoddenbruch; however, there was only one baptism of a child in 1584, probably his last, and no marriage in the parish registers. Fortunately, the author located a small book, *Trauungen Kirchspielfremder in Elberfeld (Reformed) 1585-1620 und 1649-1675*, (marriages of non-residents in the Elberfeld Reformed Church. . . .) This book contains the following record:

> 19.10.1597, Peter s [selig] Aleff's son aus dem Herenbruch im Ksp [Kirchspiel] Remschied und Geirdt Lucas Barss T [Tochter].

> 19.10.1597, Peter, deceased Aleff's son, in the Herenbruch in the parish of Remschied, and Geirdt Lucas Barss' daughter.[31]

This example clearly demonstrates patronymics were also used in some parts of Germany during the seventeenth century, although not as consistently as the Netherlands and the Scandinavian countries. In addition, a man may have taken his father-in-law's patronymic instead of his father's, for convenience or prestige.

This also illustrates the number of variants by which a man's name may be given:

> 'Peter aus dem Herenbruck im Ksp. Remscheid' became alternately known in the Elberfeld parish registers as also 'Peter auf dem Har-renbroche; Peter vom Remscheidt; Peter vom Remscheit gnat [alias] Lucas; Peter Hattenbroch; Peter Lucas; Peter vom Remsc-heit auch [also] Lucas; Peter Hattenbrock gnat Lucas; Peter in der

---

[30] REC. 117 (1986): 1.

[31] Hermann Kiessling, comp., *Trauungen Kirchspielfremder in Elberfeld [Reformed] 1585-1620 und 1649-1675* (Wuppertal-Wohwinkel: Verlag Bergisch Land der Westdeutschen Gesellschaft für Familienkunde, 1970), p. 11; FHL 1045359, it. 6.

Hattenbeck; and Petter Hudenbruck.[32]

A careful search again of the parish registers revealed a short break in the marriages from 6 August 1597 to 18 July 1601, a period of almost four years. These records disappeared from the original parish registers of Elberfeld before the Family History Library filmed the registers at Schloss Bruhl, Cologne, Germany. Therefore, the only record of the marriage of Adolph Hardenbrook's parents is found in Kiessling's book.

After finding the parents' names, the baptism of Adolph Hardenbrook, the immigrant, was easily located in the parish registers (See Illustration 3):

16 May 1599, Peter vom Remscheidt und gierdt lucas Barss dochter eheleut eine sohn gnat Aloff. Die pate Aloff Brauss und peter, peter Wilhelm's sohn. Die godt Ursel selige Gerdt pelschers dochter gnat Peinges.

16 May 1599, Peter from Remscheidt and Gierdt, Lucas Barss's daughter a legitimate son named Aloff. The godfathers Aloff Brauss and Peter, Peter Wilhelm's son. The godmothers Ursel Peinges, saintly Gerdt Pelcher's daughter.[33]

Ten Eyck-Boel Family

As stated earlier, his Amsterdam marriage intention showed that Coenradt ten Eyck was born in Moers, Germany about 1618. Moers is cataloged by the Family History Library under "Germany, Preussen, Rhineland, Moers." A search in the Reformed Church Registers of Moers reveals the following:

---

[32] REC. 117 (1986): 3.

[33] Parish Registers Reformed Church of Elberfeld, p. 271; FHL 0176329.

3 March 1617 - Wilhelm an gen Eick ein kindt getaufft genant Conradt.

3 March 1617 - Wilhelm an gen Eick had a child baptized named Conradt.[34]

The surname in this case gave some cause for caution; however, the author was assured by experienced German researchers that such archaic forms as "an gen Eick, an der Eick, and an ger Eick" were all common in that area during the seventeenth century and would have been "ten Eyck" in Dutch. Two marriages for Coenradt's father Wilhelm an gen Eick and the baptisms of two additional siblings were found in the Moers parish register.[35]

The above marriage intention of Coenradt ten Eyck in Amsterdam listed his wife Maria Boel as born in "Keulen" (in FHL catalog under Germany, Preussen, Rheinland, Cologne, now Nordrhein-Westfalen, Germany). The baptism of Maria was found in the Cologne Dutch Reformed Church parish registers as translated:

15 July 1622 was baptized a child of Tobias Boel and Grieten Apperloo, named Maria, wit.: Jeronimus Maiqvart; Marij Fromeau, wife of Nicolas Lintlau; and Marij Craij, daughter of Jacques Craij.[36]

Many entries were found for other members of the Boel family in the registers of the Reformed Churches of Cologne; however, one is especially informative (See Illustration 4):

31 Mar. 1598, Franchois Boel, Jongman, filius Adriani, van Antwerp et Elisabeth Schuts filia Diercks owch van Antwerp de bruidegom var vergezelschapt met Jasper Sonnemans de bruid var vergezelschapt met Balthasar Schuts haar broeder welke van de

---

[34] Parish Registers Reformed Church of Moers, p. 89; FHL 0489886.

[35] Ibid., pp. 42, 45, 78, 89.

[36] Parish Registers DRC of Cologne, 225: 534; FHL 0187154.

bevillings haer en de bruides getuigen geeſt.

31 March 1598, Franchois Boel, young man, son of Adrian, from
Antwerp; and Elisabeth Schuts, daughter of Dierick, also from
Antwerp; the bridegroom was assisted by Jaspar Sonnemans; the
bride was assisted by Balthasar Schuts, her brother, who gave
consent for the mother of the bride.[37]

Adrian Boel and wife Cornelia also had a child baptized
shortly after arriving in Cologne:

29 Oct. 1590, Susanna, daughter of Adriaen Boel and Cornelia. Wit:
Jan Flagelet; Catharina de huijsvrouw Denijs de Maistre; &
Emerentiana, de huijsvrowe Cornelis Boot.[38]

It is only logical to believe Adrian Boel was of an earlier
generation, since he had children born in both Cologne and
Antwerp. Therefore, he was also the father of Bartholomeus, Catharina, Tobias, and Jacques found in the Cologne
records (see "Belgium," below).

As in so many cases the Boels were victims of the Spanish
Inquisition. An edict was issued by the Spanish commander
Alexandro Farnese, Duke of Parma, in 1585, giving the
Calvinists in Antwerp four years to either revert to Catholicism or emigrate. Rather than give up the religion they so
dearly prized, thousands became refugees and sought
religious freedom on foreign soil, losing all they had except
their skills which they took with them to enrich other
cultures. The Boels chose to go to Cologne. Others fled to
the Netherlands. As many New Netherland settlers had
similar roots, the researcher will often find it necessary to
become familiar with Belgian and French records to trace
the family back to the beginning of records in Europe.

---

[37] Ibid., p. 603.

[38] Ibid., 224: 268; FHL 0187154.

Belgium

Belgian genealogy is greatly influenced by the country's geographical and historical position in Europe. As H. van Duynen says in his article "Protestantism in Belgium":

> Since this country [Belgium] is situated as a triangle between France, Germany, Holland and the North Sea, it has always been on the cross-roads of the most important European peoples; it has been, at several times, the battlefield of their armies, and it has known in different periods of its history occupation by foreign rulers.[39]

The *Encyclopaedia Britannica* has this to say concerning Belgium's history:

> Belgium came under Spanish . . . rule in 1504. In 1579 the southern Spanish provinces formed the Union of Arras (Artois), pledging allegiance to the Spanish king and Roman Catholicism. The Protestant northern provinces formed the United Provinces of the Netherlands.[40]

After their country was passed in turn from Spain to Austria, France, and the Netherlands, the Belgians finally revolted against Dutch rule in 1830, and in 1831 an independent Belgium was established under a king. In 1898 Flemish (Dutch) became an official language of Belgium along with French. Today there are two linguistic areas with different administrations.

As in most European countries, parish registers are the best genealogical source in Belgium until the eighteenth century. Due to the intense persecution of Protestants during the Inquisition, the country is predominantly Roman

---

[39] H. van Duynen, "Protestantism in Belgium," *Proceedings of the Huguenot Society of London*, 18 vols.; FHL 0990358, its. 1-7 and supp., 17: 231.

[40] *Encyclopaedia Britannica*, 1986 ed., s.v. "Belgium."

Catholic and the early registers are mostly in Latin, although French was occasionally used. There are relatively few Protestant registers, and they begin late. Protestant registers from the period relevant to New Netherland ancestors are generally lost; however, Protestant families often appear in Catholic registers.

Beginning with an edict issued by the Council of Trent in 1563 priests were required to keep registers of baptisms and marriages. Few complied with this order until after 1600, and death registers did not become general until after 1646.

Fortunately for genealogists, an act of 10 May 1865 ordered the preparation of alphabetical indexes to the registers. The results were generally commendable regardless of an attempt by a few areas, i.e. Brussels, to circumvent the act by using old indexes based on Christian names.

Regardless of their present repositories all Belgian parish registers, including their indexes, have been filmed by The Church of Jesus Christ of Latter-day Saints to be used at the Family History Library and its many centers throughout the world.

To find the town where an ancestor lived, an excellent Belgian gazetteer is *Geschieden aardrijkskundig woordenboek der Belgische Gemeente*.[41] To locate the desired parish and determine available records, see *Repertorium der Oude Parochieregisters in België* (reportory of old parish registers of Belgium).[42] With some study of the numerous abbreviations used in this work, the index will become a useful tool in the hands of the genealogist.

If the textbook for a two-year homestudy course on Belgian paleography titled *Oud schrift: kursus per briefwisseling*, referenced on page 67, has been obtained, it will provide excellent assistance in reading the old Flemish handwriting

---

[41] Eugene de Seyn, *Geschieden aardrijkskundig woordenboek der Belgische Gemeente*, 2 vols. (Turnhout: Brepols, 1941-?); n.m.

[42] Hervé Douxchamps and Raymond Tefnin, *Repertorium der oude parochieregisters in België* (Brussels: Hervé Douxchamps, 1985); n.m.

found in some Belgian parish registers.

For those who struggled through Latin in school, perhaps interpreting the old Belgian parish registers will pose no problem. However, for novices and those who wish to refresh their memory, the Family History Library has prepared the *Genealogical Word List: Latin*, which will be sent (for a nominal fee) upon request. A good dictionary in both Latin and English, such as *Cassell's New Latin Dictionary: Latin-English, English-Latin*[43] should be available at most libraries.

Examples of researching Belgian parish registers follow. As stated in the section on researching in Germany, the marriage intention of Coenradt ten Eyck and Maria Boel in Amsterdam declares she was from Cologne, Germany. In Cologne a baptism was found for Maria Boel daughter of Tobias Boel and Grieten Apperloo; a marriage intention for Franchois Boel, son of "Adrian from Antwerp, Belgium"; and the baptism of Susanna, "daughter of Adrian" suggests he was the father of Tobias, Franchois, and Susanna, as well as other Boels found in the Cologne records.

From Cologne the trail leads to Antwerp, Belgium. The parish registers of Onze Lieve Vrouw [Our Lady] Roman Catholic Church in Antwerp, list two baptisms of Adrian Boel's children which read as translated (See Illustrations 5 & 6):

28 Sept. 1567, Frans of Adrian Boel and Cornelia. Wit: Adrian de Laddrien, Jasper Somas, Apolloni van Dael, and Leske Boels.

7 Sept. 1568, Anna of Adriaen Boel and Cornelia. Wit: Franchoeys Waeschaerts [sp.?] and Ana Capellen.[44]

Although a baptism was not found for Tobias Boel,

---

[43] *Cassell's New Latin Dictionary: Latin-English, English-Latin* (New York: Funk & Wagnalls, 1959, 1968).

[44] Baptisms Onze Lieve Vrouw Roman Catholic Church of Antwerp, 1560-1569, 6: 110, 143 (verso); FHL 0296245.

circumstantial evidence established he was a member of the family of Adrian Boel from Antwerp.

Provost Family

The value of compiled family histories for providing clues to places for research, but little primary evidence or names, is very well demonstrated by Slok's article "The Provost Family in the Netherlands" found in the *Record*.[45] Although a manuscript compiled in 1725 by David Provost, entitled "A Genealogy or Short Collection of the Family of David Provost of the City and Province of New York" supplies much valuable material, Slok says in his assessment of this collection:

> While most statements in the manuscript concerning members of the Provost and Ten Waert [the mother's line] families in America can be substantiated, the European part of their history has remained shrouded and vague. The first suspicion of an inaccurate statement in the "History" concerned the surname Provost, which is purely Dutch or Flemish; or the French spelling would be Prevost . . . .[46]

After investigating the European records Slok reveals the earliest identifiable Provost was Guilliame, Guilliaem, Ghiliame, Giljaem, Willem, as he was variously known in the Roman Catholic Church parish registers of Antwerp. He married in Sint [St.] Walburgis' Church in early June 1556 Maria Karmen/Karremen, who died before October 1564. They had two daughters, Maijcken and Elijsabeth, whose birthdates have not been found since the baptisms at Antwerp did not commence until 1564.

On 17 October 1564 "Ghiliam Provoest" and Maeijken

---

[45] Hendrik O. Slok, "The Provost Family in the Netherlands," REC. 113 (1982): 1-9.

[46] Ibid., p. 2.

Stevens were married in St. Walburgis' Roman Catholic Church.[47] However, space prohibits the inclusion of this document. According to Slok:

> Guilliame was a merchant and resided in the business quarter of the city [Antwerp]. He and his wife belonged to the then secret Protestant movement, and it seems that they attended the underground Reformed Church named "De Brabantsche Olijfbergh" [The Brabant's Mount of Olives], but, to avoid the Inquisition, they, as was the custom with most Protestants in this region and time period, had their children baptized in the Roman Catholic Church of St. Walburgis in their neighborhood.[48]

Due to the persecution of Protestants during the Inquisition (already discussed), the Provost household evidently left Antwerp around 1576, as no further mention is made of their family in the records after that date. All indications suggest the Provosts moved to nearby Middleburg in the Province of Zeeland. Their activities there are difficult to trace as the church and civil records were all destroyed in May of 1943 when the archives were bombed.

The path now leads to Amsterdam where the first Provost family member found on record is Hans Mertens, husband of Maijcken Provost, the oldest daughter of Guilliame by his first wife. Mertens became a citizen of that city in 1581. Then between 1602 and 1604 the rest of the surviving members of the Provost family joined them in Amsterdam. Guilliame was a sponsor at the baptism of his grandson Guilliame on 16 August 1604[49] and had his will recorded on 28 August 1606 by Notary Heijline. He was still alive on 20 March 1607 when he attended his daughter Katharina in her marriage intention.

---

[47] Marriages Sint Walburgis Roman Catholic Church of Antwerp, 1527-1600; FHL 0296308.

[48] REC. 113 (1982): 2.

[49] Baptisms Oudekerk of Amsterdam, 4: n.p.; FHL 0113132.

Slok goes on to give a detailed account of Guilliame's children, and a few grandchildren, among whom is David Provost, son of Wilhelmus/Guilliame Provost Jr. He married Margrieta Jellis on 10 August 1637 in Amsterdam.[50] They had ten children, nine baptized in the New York Dutch Church and one born before extant records there began in 1639. In his account of the family Slok infers David Provost was the only descendant of Guilliame emigrating to New Netherland, whereas the genealogy compiled by the later David Provost (mentioned at the beginning of this account) says two of Guilliame's grandsons, David and Elias, came to America.

Thus it becomes evident finding and researching the early indexed parish registers of Belgium is far from impossible, providing the records are still extant. And tracing an ancestor to the beginning of these records brings a real sense of accomplishment.

Should a researcher be fortunate enough to read French or Flemish (Dutch will probably suffice for the latter), some other original records on film at the Family History Library will be useful. The library has the research paper *Major Genealogical Record Sources for Belgium* which can be purchased for a nominal fee or used on microfiche at a family history center in the area. The introduction says:

> The major sources are listed, together with type of record, period covered, type of information given, and source availability.[51]

France

The next country to be discussed is France. As in Belgium the most compelling reason for the exodus of

---

[50] Marriages Nieuwekerk of Amsterdam, 990: n.p. FHL 0113359.

[51] *Major Genealogical Record Sources in Belgium*; FHL G: 3, MF 6000062.

thousands from France during the Reformation period was the religious persecution of Protestants. This occurred first in the northern provinces of Artois (now Pas-de-Calais), Flanders (now Nord), and Picardy (now Somme). These people were referred to as Huguenots and Walloons and make up the majority of one's French ancestors migrating to the shores of New Netherland in the seventeenth century.

Again, the best genealogical source in France for this time period is the Roman Catholic Church parish registers. Written in Latin, the earliest start after the 1563 Council of Trent, which issued an edict that registers of baptisms and marriages were to be kept. However, it was not until the royal Ordinance of Blois in 1579 that most registers of marriages and burials were made in France. Unfortunately, since then many have perished.

Most of the extant parish registers in the Department of Nord have been microfilmed by the FHL, while a filming project is currently underway for Pas-de-Calais. To assist the researcher, occasionally a portion of these registers has been indexed and transcribed, such as the Baptisms of the Roman Catholic Church of Armentières, (Nord), 1590-1621.[52]

The parish registers are generally in poor condition and difficult to read. Some pages are seemingly written in "disappearing" ink. However, with a little practice and self-discipline, the legible ones may be read, using the Latin word list and handwriting tips mentioned in chapter 3. Nevertheless, many of the words are badly spelled and require an active imagination to decipher.

To begin, one needs a good gazetteer of the towns and departments of France. The next step is to locate the place on a map. These goals may be accomplished by using the *Bottin des Communes* (a directory of towns).[53]

Some departments of France have published inventories

[52] Baptisms Roman Catholic Church of Armentères, 1590-1621; FHL 1122756.

[53] *Bottin des Communes* (Paris: Didot-Bottin, 1988); n.m.

of the ancient parish registers existing for each town. These can be located by checking in the Family History Library Catalog under "France," the "Department," then "Inventories." The one the author used for Pas-de-Calais is available on film from the Family History Library.[54]

Protestant records also begin in the sixteenth century, but are very rare, since the records were illegal until 1789. Therefore, many Protestants are recorded in Catholic registers, as marriage by a Catholic priest was required to inherit property. The marriage of the couple will usually be found in the bride's home parish. Also children were occasionally baptized in the Catholic Church to allay suspicion the parents were "heretics." Burials were done in secret on private property, not in church burial grounds; therefore, they will not be found in Roman Catholic Church parish registers.

The conditions of these early Protestant congregations is well expressed by Harold John Grimm in *The Reformation Era, 1500-1650*:

> Those who could not flee to Switzerland or Germany formed small, compact groups that met in secret, worshipped in accordance with Protestant doctrines, and studied the Bible as well as the increasing amount of Calvinist literature that was being brought to them. As these congregations grew in size, they were sent fearless ministers trained in Geneva who preached to the faithful bands in private homes, open fields, woods, and all sorts of out-of-the-way places.[55]

Blanchan-Joire Family

In 1980 the author was in correspondence with Ruth P. Heidgerd of New Paltz, New York, concerning a mutual

---

[54] Registers Paroissiaux Etat-Civil Tables Decennales; FHL 1457263, it. 1.

[55] Harold John Grimm, *The Reformation Era, 1500-1650*, (New York: Macmillan Co., 1973), pp. 292-93; n.m.

ancestor Matthew Blanchan. She included a copy of all Blanchan and Crispel entries in the French Church of Mannheim, Baden-Württemburg, Germany, which records she had transcribed, translated, and cross referenced for the Huguenot Historical Society of New Paltz. Mannheim was one of several towns where the Blanchans took refuge on their long, circuitous route to America.

Included was the marriage "Anthoine Crispel, young man, native of St. Guin [formerly French Flanders, now Sainghin-en-Weppes, Nord, France] in the low country, and Marie Blanchan, native of Armentières [formerly in French Flanders, now Nord, France], were married in this church the 31 January, 1660."

A booklet which she also enclosed, *Matthew Blanchan in Europe and America*, says:

> According to his testamentary deposition given below (p. 15) Matthew was born at Neuville-au-Cornet, parish of Ricame . . . . Sometime before 1635 he moved to Armentières, very near the Belgian border and married Magdeleine Jorisse or Joire.[56]

Since their daughter Maria was born in Armentières it was logical to believe her parents may have married there, and that was Magdalena Joire's home parish. A search of the Baptisms of the Roman Catholic Church turned up the baptism of Magdelena:

> 27 Oct. 1611, die baptizata est Magdalena filia Petri Joire, susceptor fuit Bartholomeus Le Blanc, susceptrix fuit Magdalena Gruson.

> 27 Oct. 1611, was baptized Magdalena daughter of Petrus [Pierre] Joire, godfather Bartholomeus Le Blanc, godmother Magdalena

---

[56] Major Louis Dubois, *Matthew Blanchan in Europe and America*. Revised and enlarged by Ruth P. Heidgerd (New Paltz, New York: Dubois Family Association, Huguenot Historical Society, 1979), p. 1.

Gruson.[57]

The baptisms of five additional children were located in the same parish. The baptism of the first child Maria 1 October 1601 also gave the name of the mother as Jacoba Le Blanc.[58] Another exciting find was the marriage of Matthew Blanchan and Magdalena Joire (See Illustration 7):

15 Oct. 1633 Cont. Mat., Mattheus blanchart et Mag la Joire test. Petrus Joire et Michaele de lestre.

15 Oct. 1633 contracted marriage, Mattheus Blanchart and Magdelana Joire, witnesses Petrus Joire and Michaele De Lestre.[59]

Also the baptismal record of an additional child of this couple, who probably died young and was thus heretofore unknown, was discovered in the baptisms (See Illustration 8):

14 Aug. 1642, baptizatus fuit Maximilianus Blanchart filuis Mathei et Magdelenae Joire. Pubr. Maximilianus Lalau, et Joanna Cousmart.

14 Aug. 1642, was baptized Maximilianus Blanchart son of Matheus and Magdalena Joire. Godparents Maximilianus Lalau, and Joanna Cousmart.[60]

After ascertaining the surname a study of the *Dictionnaire Etymologique des Noms de Famille et Prénoms de France* (a

---

[57] Baptisms Roman Catholic Church of Armentères, 1590-1621, #3001; FHL 1122756.

[58] Ibid., #2808.

[59] Marriages Roman Catholic Church of Armentères, 1630-1736; FHL 1122754.

[60] Baptisms Roman Catholic Church of Armentères, 1640-1648; FHL 1133313.

dictionary of the origin of French surnames and given names) will be very helpful in recognizing the many variations names were given before they became standardized. Also many clues concerning regional origin are often included.[61]

For instance, the name "Joire" is an archaic form of "George,"[62] and "Blanc" and "Blanche" are the masculine and feminine forms of the adjective "white or fair."[63] The many variations of the latter include even "Blanchon" which is probably the origin of Matthew Blanchan's surname. For a complete study of the Joire family the researcher is referred to the article "Magdalena Joire: A 'Mademoiselle from Armentières."[64]

Duryea Family

An example of establishing a New Netherland ancestor in France is supplied by Harry Macy, Jr. in his article for the *Record* "New Light on the Origin of Joost Duryea."[65] When taking the oath of allegiance to King James II in 1687 at Bushwick, Long Island "Josst durie" indicated that he had

---

[61] Albert Dauzat, *Dictionnaire Étymologique des Noms de Famille et Prénoms de France.* Reviewed and enlarged by Marie Thérèse Morlet (Paris: Larousse, 1980).

[62] Ibid., 345.

[63] Ibid., 46.

[64] Gwenn F. Epperson, "Magdalena Joire: A Mademoiselle from Armentières," REC. 122 (1991): 85-87, reprinted as Appendix D in this guide.

[65] Harry Macy, Jr., "New Light on the Origin of Joost Duryea," REC. 121 (1990): 34-35.

been in this country for twelve years or since 1675.[66] Therefore, he was not on the accounts for passenger lists of the
Dutch West India Company. However, an article in the
Record reveals Duryea previously lived at Mannheim,
suggesting a French Huguenot background.[67]

Additional information supplied by Harold D. Duryee in
The Charles Duryee Family, published by him in 1955,
includes the marriage record of Joost Duryea and Magdalena
Le Febre or Madeleine Le Fevre on 28 February 1672 in the
Mannheim French Congregation. A more detailed version
of the same marriage record, with names of Joost's and
Magdalena's parents, was published in *The Huguenot Histo-
rian* (The Huguenot Society of New Jersey):

> 28 February 1672, Joses du Rieus, son of Simon du Rieus and
> Adriene Roul; Magdeleine le Fevre, daughter of Anthoine le Fevre
> and Anthoinette Vilain.[68]

By looking at Mannheim records of Joost's *siblings*, Mr.
Macy learned that they came from Santes near Lille. This
was previously unknown.[69]

In the section of the *Record* entitled "Additions & Correc-
tions" in October 1990, Mr. Macy adds that the Catholic
parish register of Santes, Nord, France contains the marriage
record of Joost Duryea's parents on 23 May 1663:

> Solemniter Matrimonio coniuncti fuerunt Simon Du Rietz et
> Adriana Raou presentibus Petro Le Febure et Antonio Burelle.[70]

---

[66] DHNY 1: 660; FHL 0896505.

[67] REC. 11 (1880): 62.

[68] The Huguenot Society of New Jersey, *The Huguenot Historian, 1980-
82*: 11.

[69] REC. 121 (1990): 35.

[70] Marriages Roman Catholic Church of Santas; FHL 1135031.

Mr. Macy comments:

> This bride and groom have the same names as the parents of the
> immigrant Joost Duryea, but by 1663 Joost and all his siblings had
> probably already been born. From a study of the register it appears
> very unlikely that there might have been two couples with the same
> names in this small community; it therefore seems possible that this
> 1663 ceremony took place to legitimize a Protestant marriage in the
> eyes of the state, perhaps to permit the family to depart for Mann-
> heim where they were settled by 1666. . . . It is likely that their
> children were baptized only in a Protestant church for which
> records may not have survived.[71]

Scandinavia

Another sizeable group which emigrated to New Netherland, many through Amsterdam, was the Scandinavians.

John O. Evjen, in his *Scandinavian Immigrants in New
York, 1630-1674*, identifies almost two hundred Norwegian,
Danish and Swedish immigrants to New Netherland.[72] Most
of his biographic information on these people is found in
New Netherland records, from which he identifies and describes their places of origin. In a few cases Evjen mistaken-
ly includes Dutchmen or Germans among Scandinavians, but
there are also a few Scandinavian New Netherlanders whom
he overlooks.

Scandinavia is made up of five independent nations,
Norway, Denmark, Sweden, Finland, and Iceland. However,
the preponderance of Scandinavian settlers of New Netherland were from Norway, Denmark, and Sweden. Therefore,
this study will be limited to these countries.

Although there are numerous excellent research guides

---

[71] REC. 121 (1990): 239.

[72] John Oluf Evjen, *Scandinavian Immigrants in New York, 1630-1674*
(Minneapolis: K.C. Holter Publishing Co., 1916. Reprint. Baltimore:
Genealogical Publishing Co., 1972); FHL 1033525, it. 3.

and sources available for Scandinavia, few apply to the time period covered in this work. As in other European countries the best genealogical source before civil registration is the church records and most of these start in the late 1680's. The exception is Denmark whose parish registers begin generally around 1645. Even these earliest church records are too late to include most settlers coming with the Dutch West India Company.

Regarding the church records of Denmark, *The Library* has this to say:

> The Evangelical Lutheran Church is the official church of Denmark with about 97 percent of the people belonging, but there is complete freedom of religion. . . .
> Lutheran parish registers date back to as early as 1573 and all are available on microfilm. . . . Generally they begin around 1645.[73]

Bradt Family

Although early Scandinavian church registers are scarce, some progress can be made by establishing family connections in Amsterdam. A good example is the case of Albert Andriessen Bradt whose life in New Netherland is competently covered in Evjen's book which says that "Albert Andriessen, or Albert Andriessen Bradt [Bratt], was one of the earliest Norwegian settlers in New Netherland. He came from Fredrikstad, a town at the mouth of the Glommen, the largest river in Norway."[74]

Evjen continues:

---

[73] Johni Cerny and Wendy Elliott, *The Library* (Salt Lake City: Ancestry Publishing Co., 1988); n.m.

[74] John Oluf Evjen, *Scandinavian Immigrants in New York, 1630-1674* (Minneapolis: K.C. Holter Publishing Co., 1916. Reprint. Baltimore: Genealogical Publishing Co., 1972); FHL 1033525, it. 3.

The name of Albert Andriessen occurs for the first time in a
document bearing the date 26 August 1636, an agreement between
him and two others on the one hand, and the patroon of the colony
of Rensselaerswyck, Kiliaen van Rensselaer, on the other. The
agreement was made and signed in Amsterdam.[75]

An account of the earlier life of Albert Andriessen Bradt
and his family in Amsterdam is picked up in an article for
the *Record*, "Bradt Records from Amsterdam" contributed by
Robert G. Cooney, Jr., researched and written by Harry
Macy, Jr., F.A.S.G.[76] The article gives the marriage intention
(with translation) for Albert Andriessen and Annetie Baerents:

27 March 1632
*Compareerde alsvooren Albert Andriess van Frerickstadt, varengezel,
out 24 jaere, geen ouders, wonende aande Romboutsteegh, geast met
Lourens Pieters, zijn oom en Annetie Baerents van Oudenbrath geast
met gessel baerens haer moeder wonende in Schaepensteegje, out 24
jaere.* Appeared as before mentioned, Albert Andriess from Frerickstadt, sailor, aged 24 years, no parents, living on the Romboutsteegh [street in Amsterdam], assisted by Lourens Pieters, his uncle,
and Annetie Baerents from Oudenbrath,[77] assisted by Gessel Baerens, her mother, living in Schaepensteegje, aged 24 years. (FHL
0113194, Marriage Intentions for all Dutch Reformed Churches in
the City of Amsterdam 1630-2.)

As might be expected, the marriage took place in Amsterdam's Lutheran Church, and the baptisms of two children
were found there.

Mr. Macy continues:

---

[75] Ibid.

[76] Harry Macy, Jr., "Bradt Records from Amsterdam," REC. 118
(1987): 133.

[77] This reading of the bride's native place was incorrect. She came
from *Oudenbroek* which is Altenbruch, Germany; REC. 123 (1992): 17.

On 26 August 1636 at Amsterdam, "Albert Andriessen van frederickstadt, 29 years of age, tobacco planter," signed a contract with Kiliaen van Rensselaer to emigrate to New Netherland. The log of the ship *Rensselaerswyck* shows that it sailed from Amsterdam 25 September 1636, and on 2 November in a storm off the English coast "a child was born on the ship and named and baptized in England *stoerm*; the mother is annetie baernts."[78]

Concerning the opportunities for further European research, Mr. Macy reports:

> It is generally agreed that Fre[de]rickstadt was Fredrikstad in Norway, south of Oslo; the other possibility is Friedrichstadt in Schleswig-Holstein, but Albert was frequently called 'de Noorman' (the Norwegian) in New Netherland records, and he later used the surname Bradt, which is known in Norway. It is apparently unlikely that Norwegian records can be found that would shed further light on Albert, but possibly there is more to be learned from sources in the Netherlands.[79]

Should the reader desire to continue genealogical research in the Scandinavian countries, although vital records are scarce before 1800 as stated above, there are many excellent guides available. These include brochures published by the Family History Library in its *Major Genealogical Record Sources, Series D.* An outstanding research outline for Norway is now also available with other countries soon to follow.

The advantage of these research papers is their easy accessibility at all family history centers throughout the country and directly by mail. The address is given in chapter 3.

For genealogical study in all Scandinavian countries the author suggests *Searching for Scandinavian Ancestors at the Genealogical Society Library [Family History Library]* by

---

[78] Ibid.

[79] Ibid., 133-34.

Henry E. Christiansen.[80] This book includes many sources which can be used at the centers and is on both microfilm and microfiche. Henry E. Christiansen is a very astute researcher and held an important position with the Family History Department of The Church until his retirement some years ago.

A useful aid for beginning Norwegian research is *Genealogical Guidebook and Atlas of Norway* by Frank Smith and Finn A. Thomsen.[81]

One of the research guides for Denmark used most frequently at the Family History Library is *Genealogical Guidebook and Atlas for Denmark*, also by Frank Smith and Finn A. Thomsen.[82] This work is now on microfiche for use at the family history centers.

A good book with which to start Swedish research is *Cradled in Sweden: A Practical Help to Genealogical Research in Swedish Records* by Carl-Erik Johansson.[83]

---

[80] Henry E. Christiansen, *Searching for Scandinavian Ancestors at the Genealogical Society Library* (Salt Lake City: Genealogical Society of The Church of Jesus Christ of Latter-day Saints, 1969); FHL 0897215, it. 4, MF 6039338.

[81] Frank Smith and Finn A. Thomsen, *Genealogical Guidebook and Atlas of Norway* (Logan, Utah: Everton Publishers, 1974); MF 6030098.

[82] Frank Smith and Finn A. Thomsen, comps., *Genealogical Guidebook and Atlas of Denmark* (Bountiful, Utah: Thomsen's Genealogical Center, 1986); MF 6054631.

[83] Carl-Erik Johansson, *Cradled in Sweden: A Practical Help to Genealogical Research in Swedish Records* (Logan, Utah: Everton Publishers, 1972); MF 6030093-5.

5 CONCLUSION

There is still much to be accomplished in identifying the ancestors of New Netherland settlers. The work will never be completed until *all* are accounted for and their stories told. As use is made of available records, other sources will be discovered and new electronic systems developed to speed the work. It is the responsibility of each family to go forth with fervent zeal to complete their part in this tremendous effort.

Family history research can also have a tremendous impact on human relationships. By teaching all are part of a huge family, it is possible many artificial boundaries will disappear, and the thought of lifting a hand against a nation of "relatives" will become repugnant. Then there will indeed be "peace on earth, good will to men." It is hoped this guidebook will convince the reader that family history research in the old records is both possible and rewarding.

Appendix A

The Dutch Ancestry of the Van Barkello Family in Early Kings County, New York; in the Netherlands, by Hendrik O. Slok.

THE NEW YORK
Genealogical and Biographical Record
VOL. 115 OCTOBER 1984 NUMBER 4

THE DUTCH ANCESTRY OF THE VAN BARKELLO FAMILY IN EARLY KINGS COUNTY, NEW YORK; IN THE NETHERLANDS[1]

By Hendrik O. Slok

In our country, there are presently quite a number of individuals with the surname VanBarkeloo, or a derivative thereof. Such are likely descendants of two brothers named Willem and Harmen Jansz or Jansen[2] surnamed Van Berckeloo who arrived in this country from the Netherlands in the middle of the seventeenth century, and settled on Long Island. By the eighteenth century their descendants had spread throughout New York, New Jersey, Pennsylvania and Maryland.

In THE RECORD (77:31 and 84:70&196) are two articles concerning their descendants in the seventeenth and eighteenth centuries in the before-mentioned states. The articles were written by the competent researcher William J. Hoffman, F.G.B.S.

This article is meant as a follow up and deals with such American background as is relevant for searchers in the Netherlands records.

It is presumed that Willem Jansz van Berckeloo was in this country by the fall of 1657, possibly earlier. He resided at first in Flatbush (Vlakebosch) in the present Borough of Brooklyn. On 23 June 1662 he bought a house, barn and lot of land at Gravesend, an English settlement.[3] His marriage took place just prior to or on 3 February 1658 as an entry in the Dutch Reformed Church deacons' accounts of Flatbush have it:[4] "received the marriage fee for Anthony Jansen's daughter, 6 Guilders".[5] Her name was Cornelia Anthonisd- the daughter of Anthony Jansz alias "de Turck," from Fez or Salee in Morocco, a colorful character and Grietje or Geertje Reijnsd. Willem Jansz van Berckeloo and his wife are listed as members in the records of the Dutch Reformed Church of New York City (Nieuw Amsterdam), list of 1649–1660 as Willem Janszen and Cornelia Anthonis his housewife.[6]

---

[1] Searches made in September 1975
[2] The appendage Jansz signifies a patronymic or father's name. The surname van Berckeloo is derived from the place of origin, the present day Borculo. See the research paper I wrote for the Genealogical Society of Utah on the subject: Research Paper C Series No. 28
[3] Notary S. la Chaire records HSYB 1900: 145
[4] Hereafter referred to as DRC
[5] Flatbush DRC GS microfilm No. 1.016.561 item 2.
[6] NYC DRC Membership records. He signs his name as Willem Jansz van borkello.

Harmen Jansz van Berckeloo, his brother, arrived in this country during May 1662 on the ship *de Trouw*, with a wife and two children, ages 5 and 3 years.[7]

That these two men were brothers can be proven by the fact that they both had the same patronymic and surname, the latter of which they added when on these shores. Definite proof is found in the records of Notary Salomon la Chaire at New York City, a declaration dated 22 June 1662, concerning a gunner they met on the boat from Medemblicq to Amsterdam "Harmen Jansen van Barkeloo and Willem Jansen van Barkeloo, brothers, declared that they in February of the present year traveled, etc."[8] From this statement we know that Willem Jansz was back in the Netherlands to fetch his brother Harmen and visited the area where he was born. It is possible that they also accompanied Stoffel Smet from Ruurlo and Adriaen Hendricksz from Borculo in February 1662.[9,10a]

The route they likely took from the Borculo area: West to Zutphen, then northwest along the frozen IJsselriver to Kampen, from there across the Zuiderzee to Medemblik [present spelling]; then South to Amsterdam, where they stayed for nearly a month; from Amsterdam by boat to the Isle of Texel where the ship *de Trouw* was anchored to await favorable winds, and left there on 24 March 1662, crossed the North Sea to the south of England, then by southern or winter route crossing the Atlantic just north of Bermuda, then past the coast of Virginia and north to New York (Nieuw Nederland). Such voyages usually took from 6 to 8 weeks.

The name of Harman's wife can be found in the joint will of her second husband, Hans Harmansz; she is referred to as Willemtjen Warnaers also surnamed Eldringh elsewhere in the records. In this document her children by Harmen Jansz, her first husband, named Jannetje, Reynier, Harmen and Jan Harmensz van Berckeloo, Willem Van Berckeloo were to receive a legacy. In the will, dated 12 November 1694,[11] Willempje's patronymic is Warnaers. The first two children mentioned in the ships listing are Jannetje and Reynier, born respectively about 1657 and 1659 in the Netherlands.

All the before mentioned information formed the basis for research in the Borculo [present spelling] area records in the province of Gelderland, the Netherlands. However, one should be aware of the fact that in that area predominantly Saxon traditions existed which had also a bearing on the language and therefore in the spelling of given names and surnames. Surnames are usually derived from farmsteads, parcels of land, manor houses, hamlets, etc. Both given and surnames in New Netherland from the northern Frisian

[7] Ship accounts of WIC of passengers owing money.
[8] Notary S. la Chaire records HSYB 1900: 144
[9] Letter to Gov Peter Stuyvesant dated 4 Feb. 1662 at Amsterdam Dutch Mss Correspondence XIV: 56
[10a] The present spelling of the records mentioned: Reurlo and Borculo.

and eastern Saxon provinces in the Netherlands are often standardized to Holland-Dutch, the official language of the West India Company.[10b]

Searches in the Borculo DRC records 1653–1663 failed to disclose any information concerning Willem or Harmen Jansz and wife. The expression "van (from) Borculo" could also refer to the Jurisdiction- Court Jurisdiction of Borculo which contains the villages and hamlets, some with their own churches, of Geesteren, Geeselaer, and Haarlo.

Investigation of the Geesteren DRC records contained the following interesting entries: (G.S. film No. 108.713)

Membership records, list made up in 1655: *Harmen* Lubberdinck[12] & vrou, added later, *verreist nae nieu Nederlandt (Harman* Lubberdinck & wife, *traveled to new Nederland.)*

Baptismal record 1652 onwards:

27 April 1656: Harman Lubberdinck's en *Willemken's* dochter *Jenneke* gedoopt, getuijgen: *Warner Elderinck*, Geesken Lubberdinck & Otjen Mols

(translation)

Harmen Lubberdinck's and *Willemken's* daughter *Jenneke* baptized, witnesses: *Warner Elderinck,* Geesken Lubberdinck & Otjen Mols

5 June 1659: *Harmen Lubberdinck's* and *Willemken's* son *Reint* baptized. Witnesses: the Noble squire Reiner van Duithe named Buth toe Mensinck, *Jan Lubberdinck the Elder* and Griete Mols.

Marriages, 1652 onwards:
27 March 1653:
Harmen Lubberdinck son of *Jan Lubberdinck* from Geesteren
with
Willemken Elderinck daughter of *Warner Elderinck* from Hengelo and married there 11 April.

When these entries are compared with what is known from American sources, little doubt is left as to the identity of these individuals:

Harman Jansz Lubberdinck and wife Willemken Warners Elderinck and children Jenneke (Jannetje) and Reint (Reynier) ages 5 and 3 years, traveled to New Netherland after 1655.

In the Hengelo DRC baptismal records, the entry of the first born child of this couple was registered: 27 March 1654, *Harman Jans Lubberdinck* & *Willemken Warnaers* a daughter named *Jenneken* was baptized, witnesses Henrick Waerle, Henrick ten Holte, his daughter Reyntie, his wife and sister. This child must have died soon afterwards.

It is known from American sources that Willem, like his brother Harmen, had also a daughter named Jannetje, who keeping in mind the Dutch naming custom, was no doubt named after her paternal grandmother. This was confirmed by the following marriage entry found in the Geesteren DRC:[13]

[10b] A classic example is Jan Jacobsz alias de Vries of Kings County. As his alias indicates he is a Frisian. His Frisian name was Jentie Jeppes.
[12] Lubbeerdinck, a farmstead on which they resided for several generations, is located southeast of Geesteren. In America, this very local name was superseded by *van Barculoo.*
[13] GS. No. 108.713

Jan Lubberdinck, widower of the late Janneken Aelinckhave from Geesteren.

with

Geesken Roosinck, daughter of the late Aerent Roosinck from Mallen were married 6 November 1653 at Geesteren. The baptismal records list four children of this couple:

Jan	24 February 1654
Arent	4 November 1655, this child died before 1660
Berentje	5 July 1657
Arent	9 September 1660

The Geesteren DRC records commence in 1652; it was therefore not possible to obtain the baptismal dates for Willem and Harmen. However from various entries found in the baptismal and marriage records a fair idea could be formed as to other relatives, brothers and sisters, of these men, children of Jan Lubberdinck and Jenneken Aelinckhave:

Bernt Jansz	born about 1618, listed as witness
Willem Jansz	born about 1621, removed to New Netherland
Jan Jansz	born about 1623, married Reintje Moll; they had seven children
Harman Jansz	born about 1626, married Willemken Elderinck
Gerrit Jansz	born about 1629, married 15 October 1654, Geesken Jans & Bruininck
Geertruijdt Jansd	born about 1633, married 23 January 1670, Jan Hendricksz Roosinck

Searches in the nearby town of Lochem DRC[14] revealed the marriage entry of Jan Lubberdinck's first marriage:
2 April 1617:

Jan Lubberdinck son of Bernt Lubberdinck, youngman from Giestren.
with
Jennicken ten Olinchave, daughter of Willem ten Olinchave,
young daughter from Lochem, married at Giestren.[15]

From this it can be stated that Willem Jansz our emigrant was named after his maternal grandfather. In the Borculo District Court records we find this couple listed as *Johan Lubberdinck* and *Janneken* his wife on 23 April 1638 when they agree to pay 100 daalders (150 guilders) to Johan van Delden and wife, that they had borrowed, by May of 1639.[16] It is in these records that the will of Jan's parents was located. On 8 November 1627 appeared *Bernt Lubberdinck and his wife Toniske*; they make this instrument a will to the longest living, as *momber* (guardian or testator) they appoint Hermanus van Keppel; children were to receive equal portions of their estate. No children are mentioned by

[14] GS No. 108.768; 896.364
[15] The spelling of names and place names are often in local dialect
[16] Court records Volume 397 folio 73 GS. No. 595.718

name.[17] Hermanus van Keppel seems to be a relative, perhaps related to Toniske. The DRC records of Lochem commence in the fall of 1582. Searches revealed the entries of five children of Willem ten Olinckhave; his name is also spelled Aelinckhave and Oellinckhave.[18]

Geertruijdt	15 June 1585	
Dercksken	17 Jan. 1590	No wife's name or witnesses are listed
Jennecken	17 Jan. 1592	who married Jan Bernts Lubberdinck
Gerrijt	29 Aug. 1593	
Anna	11 Jan. 1596	

The Lochem court records series: Transports—Transfer of properties, wills, settlements, etc.[19] contains a settlement of an estate dated December 1608. It names Willem ten Olinckhave and his wife Nanne ten Bijler daughter of the late Tonnis ten Bijler and Johanne Hovels, also two sons, not listed in the baptismal records, named in this document as Tonnis and Harmanus ten Olinckhave, probably born in 1582 and 1587 respectively.

In the Court records series: Civil cases, Willem ten Olinckhave testifies in June 1613, his age listed as 68 years old. He was born in 1545. The records further show that he was Mayor of Lochem over the years 1607–1630. The last reference of him was made on 8 March 1630. He was dead by 20 May 1630. His wife Nanne ten Bijler was deceased by February 1626.[20]

Lochem was in 1582 battle frontline territory: the war of Independence against Spain was in full force (1568–1648). The Spanish troops had the town surrounded; the countryside was pillaged. The church at Geesteren became a place of refuge for the population in the general area. On 23 September 1582 the siege of Lochem was lifted but the Spanish troops remained in the south and northeast of the county of Zutphen in which both places are located. In 1587 the Dutch troops leveled all buildings of major size, which included the church of Geesteren, in order to prevent the enemy from using it as fortification. In 1609 the twelve-year truce became effective and daily life could more or less continue in a normal fashion. After 1621 the hostilities resumed. In 1627 the last Spanish stronghold in the region, the town of Grol, was liberated and the rebuilding of dikes, roads, houses and farms could begin in earnest. The restoration of the church at Geesteren began in 1627. In that year, the court records of Borculo district commenced.[21]

Hengelo, located southwest of Ruurlo and Borculo, is the village where Willemke Warnaers Elderinck was born about 1630. The DRC records commence in 1642, too late to locate her baptismal entry. Her parents are listed

[17] ditto Volume 395 folio 31 GS. No. 595.718; Jan Lubberdinck is temporary poor master of the DRC at Geesteven 10 July 1628 Volume 396 folio 71 verso.
[18] GS. No. 108.768; 897.353
[19] GS No. 861.289; 861.290; 861.291
[20] GS No. 861.277; 861.278
[21] Gelre: bijdragen en mededelingen 1932 Volume XXXV:154

on various occasions as witnesses as Warnaer Elderinck op het Beeckvelt and Willemke, his wife, nothing more. The Court records commence in 1667 — also too late to trace them. Further searches in the Court records of the before mentioned places may reveal more information, but the searches in them are tedious, they are not indexed, some are water damaged, the ink in many places is faded, the handwriting is often difficult to read, quite sloppy half of the time, and a page-by-page search is required.

TRANSCRIPTION OF ENTRIES:

Membership Listing 1655. DRC Geesteren

1. Harmen Lubberdinck & Vrou Verreist
          nae nieu Nederlandt
  Jan Lubberdinck d'olde & Vrou
  Jan Luberdinck dejonge & Vrou

Marriage rec's. 1653 DRC Geesteren

2. October
    Den 9
          Jan Lubberdinck wedeman[22] van Zall[23] Jeneken
          Aelinckhave uijt Geesteren met
          Geesken Roosinck dochter van Zall Aerent
          Roosinck uijt Mallen & den 6 November binnen
          Geesteren getrout

3. Eodem[24] Harmen Lubberdinck soone van Jan Lubberdinck
          uijt Geesteren
                    met
          Willemken Elderinck dochter van Warner
          Elderinck uijt Hengelo & aldaer den 11 April
            getrout

Baptismal rec's. 1659 DRC Geesteren

4. Junius   Den 5
          Harmen Lubberdincks ende Willemkens
          Soone Reint gedoopt Get: die Weleede
          Jr:[25] Reiner van Duithe genaempt Buth toe
          Mensinck. Jan Lubberdinck de Olde ende
          Grijte Mols.

Baptismal rec's. 1592 January DRC Lockem

5. Itym[26]   17 Willem ten oellenckhave sijn
          Dochter, Jenneken

---

[22] widower
[23] Zalliger (the late)
[24] ditto
[25] joncker = squire
[26] item (ditto or the same)

Appendix B

The European Origin of the Hardenbrook Family, by Gwenn
F. Epperson.

THE NEW YORK
Genealogical and Biographical Record

VOL. 117   JANUARY 1986   NUMBER 1

THE EUROPEAN ORIGIN OF THE HARDENBROOK FAMILY

Gwenn F. Epperson

Since the article, entitled "The Hardenbrook Family," by Howard S. F. Randolph, F.G.B.S., with the short addenda, "Pre-American Research", by William J. Hoffman, F.G.B.S., appeared in THE RECORD (70:128–33 & 373–78), an in-depth study has been done which has brought to light the very interesting origin of the Hardenbrook name, as it is known today, and takes the family from Germany to Amsterdam and then to New York City.

Adolph Hardenbrook, the immigrant to New York in 1660 with wife and 26 year old son, was the pivotal character between the old and new world and establishing Elberfeld, Germany as his ancestral home was not difficult, as explained in Mr. Randolph's article, to which reference has already been made.

The real problem lay in tracing the ancestry of Adolph Hardenbrook. Although the records of the Elberfeld Reformed Church began in 1584, with only a few gaps, noting the exception of the marriages which are missing from 1620–1649 and cover the period of the Thirty Years War, the books are water-damaged, contain torn pages, suffer extreme ink bleed-through, and are poorly microfilmed. This, added to the old Gothic handwriting, archaic use of words, erratic spelling, and a mixture of patronymics and "set" surnames, all so typical of this area and time period, present a very real challenge to the genealogist.

The baptisms and marriages covering the proper time period were searched several times, keeping in mind that Adolph Hardenbrook, in the baptisms of his children, was referred to as Aloff Luckes as late as 1646. This would indicate that he was using a patronymic and his father's given name was Lucas. However, the possibility also existed, although not as likely, that the patronymic "Lucas" had become a fixed surname and Adolph had changed it to "Hoddenbruch" to distinguish it from other families by the same surname. Therefore, it was necessary that all entries for men with the given or surname "Lucas" be noted.

For some reason, the name Lucas was not popular in that area and the only name which met the requirements was that of Lucas Barss. However, the records contained only one baptism for a child of his, in 1584, probably his last, since the records began in that year. This indicated he was of a prior generation.

Since nothing noteworthy turned up in the parish registers, it was decided to refer to a small book, *Trauingen Kirschspielfremder in Elberfeld (Reformed) 1585–*

1620 und 1649–1675, compiled by Hermann Kiessling, published in 1913, for any possible clues. There on page eleven is this reference:

> 19.10.1597, Peter s [selig] Aleffs S [Sohn] aus dem Herenbruck im Ksp [Kirschspiel] Remscheid und Geirdt Lucas Barss T [Tochter].

Translation

> 19.10.1597, Peter, deceased Aleff's son, in the Herenbruck in the parish of Remscheid, and Geirdt, Lucas Barss' daughter.

At once the whole picture fell into place like a jigsaw puzzle. Obviously Peter and his children had taken the patronymic "Lucas" instead of his father's, "Aleff." Inquiry established the fact that many times this occurred if the father-in-law was well-to-do and owned property, especially when the man came from another place and his own father was deceased.

Why this entry had been overlooked in searching the microfilm copy of the marriages of Elberfeld became the pressing question. Another careful search revealed the fact that, at the bottom of page 942, after a marriage entry, dated 6 August 1597, is written in another handwriting, "bis 1601 fehlt [missing until 1601]." The next entry at the top of page 943 is incomplete, and the one after is dated 18 July 1601[1]. Therefore, this indicates that the marriages from 6 August 1597 to 18 July 1601, a period of almost four years, disappeared from the original parish registers of Elberfeld between 1913, when Mr. Kiessling compiled his book, and 1957, when the Genealogical Society of Utah filmed the registers in the archives at Schloss Bruhl. As far as has been determined at this writing, only Mr. Kiessling's book contains a reference to the marriage in question and only because the groom was a "stranger" from another parish outside of Elberfeld.

In the middle ages Remscheid was a domaine-court with many smaller dependent courts. One of these was the court of "Haddenbruch." The owner of this court was first mentiond in 1369, Henkyn van Hoddenbroke [Henke of H.]. In the 14th century the organization of the domaine-courts declined. The courts in this area became diet-courts [local representative assemblies] and the land was divided.

Out of this division arose a tiny village called "Haddenbrock," consisting of several farms which belonged to the old parish [Kirchspiel] Remscheid. In 1666 and 1675 two farms at Hoddenbrock were mentioned, and in 1818 there were six houses with 36 inhabitants. Today Haddenbruch is a small district within the town of Remscheid and is nearly unknown. However, six families or persons named Haddenbrock and three named Haddenbruch are listed in the city directory.

The name Haddenbrock consists of two parts, "Hodden or Hadden," meaning small rocks, and "brock or bruch," meaning a swampy land or meadow. A small

[1] G.S. No. 176, 330, pp. 942 & 943

brook called the "Haddenbach' [Hoddenbeke in the middle ages] flows from the area.[2]

From this point on, research on the Hardenbrook family was all downhill. "Peter aus dem Herenbruck im Ksp. Remscheid" became alternately known in the Elberfeld parish registers as also "Peter auff dem Harrenbroche; Peter vom Remscheidt; Peter vom Remscheit gnat [alias] Lucas; Peter Hattenbroch; Peter Lucas; Peter vom Remscheit auch [also] Lucas; Peter Hattenbrock gnat Lucas; Peter in der Hattenbeck; and Petter Hudenbruck." The baptisms of his children[3] are as follows:

i. Ursel, bap. 29 Apr. 1598.[4] Godmothers: Ursel, Hamen Barss' wife; and Merg, Johan's wife from Loh in the Morian. Godfather: Clemens, [illegible] Kirberig's son. Bur. 30 Apr. 1598.
ii. Aloff, bap. 16 May 1599. Godfathers: Aloff Brauss; and Peter, Peter Wilhelm's son. Godmother: Ursel, deceased Gerdt Pelscher's' daughter, alias Peinges.
iii. Judit, bap. 4 Mar. 1601. Godmother: maiden of Munst; Matteis Grihber's wife; and Trintge, Abel Katterberg's daughter. Godfather: Johanis Leutgers, alias Holstweiler, from Himssburg, now in the [illegible].
iv. Engel, bap. 28 Dec. 1603. Godfathers: Engel from Lo in the Morian; and Jaspar Schridtman. Godmother: Merg, Gerhardt Kremer's wife. Bur. 18 Jan. 1607.[5]
v. Sara, bap. 11 June 1606. Godmothers: Sara, Gerling Kniffel's wife; and Veulffing, Enngel Driess' wife [illegible]. Godfather: Johann [illegible] Kupfferschleger.
vi. Peter, bap. 26 May 1608. Godfathers: Gordert Bungen; and Wilhelm Barss. Godmother: Trintgen, decreased Johann Hunigshausen's daughter.
vii. Ursula, bap. 19 Aug. 1612. Godmothers: Grietgen, Jasper Peltzer's wife from Wieheliehaussen; and Trientgen, Engel Treiger's wife. Godfather: Johann Schlosseler in the Hausippe.

No burial entry was found for Peter vom Remscheid; however, it must have occurred after 6 September 1615, when he was named as godfather at the baptism of a child. The burial of his wife[6] is given; translation is as follows:

24 July 1630, Geirdt Luckes in the castle, of the plague.

Peter's son Aloff, or Adolph as he is now known, married twice, although neither marriage entry was found, since, unfortunately, both fell within the missing marriages of 1620–1649, as did those of his surviving brother, Peter, and his sisters. This further complicated the research, since the marriage records usually give the maiden name of the bride and name the fathers of the bride and groom.

The baptism of Alloffs Luckes' first child, no mother's name given,[7] is as follows:

[2] Ltr. fm. Dr. W. Lorenz, Archiv der Stadt Remscheid, dtd. 18 Feb. 1985.
[3] G.S. No. 176, 329, pp. 250, 271, 308, 362, 418, 470 & 586.
[4] G.S. No. 176, 330, p. 638.
[5] Ibid., p. 661.
[6] G.S. No. 176, 341, p. 41.
[7] G.S. No. 176, 331, p. 11.

i. Johann, bap. 9 Feb. 1625. Godfathers: Johan Erff's son in the Gatten; and Willem Luckes [Adolph's brother-in-law]. Godmother: Trin, Johann Keijsberig's daughter.

Then in the burials on 5 March 1625, is this entry, "Margreidta, Alloffs Luckes . . . "[8] The rest is lost in the margin. No relationship is discernible; however, it can be safely assumed she was his wife, since he had no mother or sister by that name, and children's names were rarely given in the burial records. The child died also, for on 30 March 1625, the burial of a child of Alloff Luckes is recorded.[9] Between the death of his first wife on 5 March 1625 and the baptism of his second child on 31 October 1627, Adolpf married Merig or Maria Caterberg. Although only her first name was given in two baptisms of her eight children in Elberfeld, the membership lists of the Dutch Reformed Church of New York included her maiden name between those of her husband and her son Abel on 2 October 1662 (Rec. 9:75).

The children of Adolph Hardenbrook and Maria Caterberg[10] are as follows:

i.   31 Oct 1627, "A child of Alloffs Luckers came into this world dead.[11]
+ ii.   Johannes, b. ca. 1629
iii.   Greidtgum [Margriet], bap. 18 June 1631. Godmothers: Greidtgem Trin, Abel's daughter; Greidtgum, Peter Leutterkay's wife; and Gerdt Eullenberig (see Rec. 70:129).
iv.   Eingel, bap. 24 Jan. 1633. Godfathers: M. [Meister] Eingel Katterberig, school superintendent, of this place; and Johann Kijtl.
+ v.   Driss [Andries], bap. 22 Mar. 1634. Godfathers: Driss Seijbels; and Petter Weulffding vom Lo. Godmother: Geirdrutt "auf der Auw" (more later).
+ vi.   Abel, b. ca. 1636 (more later).
vii.   Johannes Petter, bap. 4 July 1638 (no godparents given).
viii.   1 Feb 1641, "A child of Alloffs Luckes died at birth."[12]

Since nothing further was found concerning child No. 4, Eingel, it can be assumed the following burial entry[13] applied to him:

3 Oct. 1641, a son of Alloffs Luckes died in Lo's mill under a wheel.

Another burial was recorded on 23 November 1646, "A child of Allofs Hoddenbruch,"[14] and is assumed to be child No. 7, Johannes Peter, since nothing further is found concerning him either.

This leaves the known children of Adolph Hoddenbrook, appearing in later records. However, as in all research efforts, some disappointments occurred. Neither the baptism of an Abel nor a plausible Johannes, appearing in New York records as sons of Adolph, were found. Child No. 7, Johannes Peter, was born much too late to be the Johannes Hardenbrook who married Ursula

[8] G.S. No. 176, 341, p. 23.
[9] Ibid., p. 23.
[10] G.S. No. 176, 331, pp. 305, 333, 364, & 9.
[11] G.S. No. 176, 341, p. 31.
[12] Ibid., p. 99.
[13] Ibid., p. 101.
[14] Ibid., p. 113.

Teitschman or Duytsman in Elberfeld on 27 April 1654,[15] as he would have been only 15 years old, which all consulted consider highly unlikely. It can only be assumed that the two baptisms in question were omitted by the parish priest.

The children of Lucas Barss stayed in Elberfeld and retained the surname Barss, while those of his son-in-law, Peter vom Remscheid, eventually took the surname Hodenbruch in Germany which became Hardenbroeck in the Netherlands and later evolved into Hardenbrook after their emigration to America. Peter's son Peter went to Amsterdam about 1644, while his son Adolph and his children went to New York between 1659 and 1664; that is, all except his son Andries who stayed behind in Amsterdam with his uncle Peter.

The marriage intention of Andries Hardenbroeck and Aartje Jans[16] provided a gold mine of information as follows:

> 4 April 1663, Andries hardenbrock van elbervelt schoenmaker 26 jaer de vader ten niew nederlant geassisteert met zijn oom pieter hardenbroeck woont in Dirck van Arsen steegh en Aertje Jans won. A. out 25 jaer, onders doot geassisteert met haer peet Aelyje Sijbrants woont op de Noorder Marckt.
>
> s/ Andries Hardenbroeck
> s/ Aeltje Jans

Translation:

> 4 April 1663, Andries Hardenbroeck from Elberfeld, shoemaker, 26 years of age, the father in New Netherland, assisted by his uncle Pieter Hardenbroeck, living in the Dirck van Arsen Street, and Aartje Jans from Amsterdam, 25 years of age, parents are deceased, assisted by her godmother, Aelyje Sijbrants, living on the North Market.
>
> s/ Andries Hardenbroeck
> s/ Aeltje Jans

Apparently "uncle Pieter Hardenbroeck," brother of Adolph, was the first of the Hardenbrook family to establish himself in Amsterdam. He probably married Elsje Jans (later adding the surname of Wijnties) about 1644 in Elberfeld which was during the time period of missing marriage records. Their first child, Jacobus, was born in Amsterdam in 1645, according to his marriage intention;[17] however, his baptism was not found. The children of Pieter Hardenbroeck, baptisms in the Oudekerk[18] are:

i. Jacobus, b. ca. 1645, m. 5 Oct. 1681, Johanna van Rossum at Purnerende, N-Holl., Neth.[19] Bur. 13 Nov. 1691, Amsterdam, Neth.[20]
ii. Geesje, bap. 21 Jan. 1646, wit: Heindrik van Schopinge and Orselijntje Hardenbroeck.
iii. Luikas, bap. 3 Sept. 1647, wit: Pieter Gerardij and Griet Joors. Bur. 26 Jan. 1673.[21]

---

[15] G.S. No. 176, 331, p. 25.
[16] G.S. No. 113, 214, p. 55 (left).
[17] G.S. No. 113, 227.
[18] G.S. No. 113, 133.
[19] G.S. No. 113, 227.
[20] G.S. No. 113, 377.
[21] Ibid.

iv.   Abraham (twin), bap. 13 May 1649, wit: Petri Gijrardt and Judith Hardenbroeckl; d.y.
v.   Judith (twin), bap. 13 May 1649, same wit.
vi.   Jonathan, bap. 11 Dec. 1650, wit: Sara Werelt and Jonathan Werelt: m. (1) 24 Aug.
      1680, Cornelia van Grou, (2) 21 Mar. 1686, Maria Fonteijn.[22]
vii. Abraham, bap. 12 Sept. 1655, wit: Margriet Haddenbroeck.

Burials in the Old Sides Chapel of Amsterdam[23] include the following record:

> 13 May 1671, Pitter Hardenbroeck on the Reglt Canal.

The children of Andries, son of Adolph Hardenbrook and Maria Caterberg, baptisms in the Westerkerk,[24] are as follows:

i.   Joannis, bap. 8 Aug. 1664, wit: Pieter Hardenbroeck [g. uncle] and Cornelia Corneliss; d.y.
ii.   Joannis, bap. 25 Sept. 1665, wit: Goedert Ullenbergh and Geertruijt van der Heyde (see REC. 70:373).
iii. Adolph, bap. 25 Dec. 1667, wit: Adolf Hardenbroeck and Maria Hardenbroeck [grandparents].
iv.   Adolphus, bap. 31 Mar. 1669, wit: Pieter Hardenbroeck [g. uncle] and Ursula Gerradts.
v.   Pieter, bap. 13 Feb. 1671, wit: Pieter Hardenbroock and Elfien Hardenbroock [g. uncle and g. aunt].
vi.   Maria, bap. 23 Sept. 1672, wit: Pieter Hardenbroock and Elfien Hardenbroock [g. uncle and g. aunt].

Andries Hardenbroeck's burial is found in the records of the North Churchyard, Amsterdam[25] and reads:

> 14 May 1673, Andries Hardenbroek living in the Prinse's Street next to the courthouse.

That members of the Hardenbrook family made trips between Amsterdam and the New World is evidenced by their appearances as witnesses at the baptisms of family members' children in both places. Andries, son of Adolph, was a witness at the baptism of his brother Abel's child on 19 May 1669 (BDC:94) and Jonathan, son of Peter, was a witness at the baptism of this cousin Abel's child on 15 February 1671 (BDC:100).

Adolph Hardenbrook and his wife Maria Caterberg also returned to Amsterdam from New York to witness the baptism of their grandson Adolph in 1667.[26] It is not known when this couple returned to New York; however, in papers relating to the administration of Gov. Colve's estate, dated 27 September 1674, is a petition by Frederick Philips, the second husband of their daughter Margriet, "complaining that the court at Willemstadt [Albany] had taxed his father-in-law, Adolf Hardenbroeck, who is merely his agent, and as his [P's] estate is taxed in New Orange, prays that the tax in Willemstadt may be taken off." (CEM: 26)

---

[22] G.S. No. 113, 226.
[23] G.S. No. 113, 377.
[24] G.S. No. 113, 170, & 113, 171.
[25] G.S. No. 113, 382, p. 16.
[26] G.S. No. 113, 170.

Appendix C

The Ten Eyck-Boel European Connection, by Gwenn F. Epperson.

THE TEN EYCK-BOEL EUROPEAN CONNECTION *

By Gwenn F. Epperson

Regardless of the voluminous material suggesting a Dutch background for the Ten Eyck family of New York,[1] a Dutch acquaintance remarked, "Ten Eyck is not a Dutch name!" This statement started an extensive investigation into the European origin of the Ten Eyck family, which produced some surprising results and also extended the Boel line several generations.

Since Coenraet Ten Eyck, the immigrant ancestor, came to New York by way of Amsterdam, the research started there. The marriage intention of Coenraet Ten Eyck and Maria Boel[2] was found:

> 12 May 1645, Coenradt ten Eyck van Meurs schoenmakergezel wonende 11 jare op de N.Z. Voorburgwall out 27 jaren geen ouders hebben en Maria Boel van Keulen out 23 jaren wonen op de Coninxgracht, geen ouders hebbende geassisteerd met haar zuster Jannetie Boel.
> s/ Konradt ten Eyck
> s/ Maria Boel
> Dese personen zyn tot Amsterveen getrouwtr de 4 June 1645 door Symen Wilmerdonex prest. aldaar.

Translation

> 12 May 1645, Coenradt ten Eyck from Moers, shoemaker's helper, residing 11 years at the N.Z. Voorburgwal, age 27 years, parents are dead; and Maria Boel from Cologne, age 23 years, residing at the Coninxgracht, parents are dead, assisted by her sister, Jannetie Boel.
> s/ Konradt ten Eyck
> s/ Maria Boel
> These persons were married at Amstelveen 4 June 1645 by Symen Wilmerdonex, pastor there.

Amstelveen is a village five miles south of Amsterdam. Its extant Reformed Church registers do not start until 1699, therefore, no minister's record of their marriage was found, nor any additional information concerning the family.

From the marriage intention, it was learned that Coenraet Ten Eyck arrived in Amsterdam about 1634 and was indeed born in Moers, Germany, not the Netherlands, as had been supposed. However, following the migration pattern of many immigrants to New York during that time period, Coenraet was married in the Netherlands and had several children before emigrating to America.

The baptisms of Coenraet Ten Eyck's first three children, who accompanied him to New York about 1651, were found in the Dutch Reformed Church records of the Oude Kerk[3] and the Nieuwe Kerk:[4]

*(From *The New York Genealogical and Biographical Record*, Vol. 118, Number 1, Jan. 1987.)

[1] Rec. (63:142).
[2] G.S. No. 113,203, p. 48.
[3] G.S. No. 113,133, vol. 8.
[4] G.S. No. 113,146, vol. 43.

   i.   Marija, bap. 2 Apr. 1646, wit: Hendrik Boel, and Marij ten Eyck.

  ii.   Jacob, bap. 8 Aug. 1647, wit: Jacob ten Eijck.

 iii.   Deryck, bap. 27 Oct. 1648, wit: Mathijs Glas, Sijbert van Loon, and Magdalena Ruts.

On 1 August 1645, shortly after his marriage, Coenraet Ten Eyck, shoemaker from Moers, became a citizen of Amsterdam.[5]

Moers was the next place of research. The town lies immediately west of Duisberg in the lowland area of West Germany near the Dutch border, now known as the Ruhr. Moers was first mentioned in the 9th century. It developed around the castle of the Counts of Moers and was chartered about 1300. In 1601 Moers became the property of Maurice of Nassau, Prince of Orange, who fortified it. Perhaps this explains the large number of military men recorded in the old church register. In 1712 Moers passed to Prussia but is now in the province of Nordrhein-Westfalen.[6]

The Moers Reformed Church register on microfilm at the Genealogical Society library in Salt Lake City, Utah covers the years 1612 to 1636 and includes baptismal, marriage, and burial entries, recorded together each day as they occurred. Although the microfilm copy is legible, the pages were not filmed in consecutive order, creating some difficulty for the researcher.

Another problem is the many incomplete entries in the Moers Reformed Church register. Only the father's name was given in the baptismal records, and sometimes even the name and/or sex of the child was omitted. Also the marriages did not always give the names of the individuals — merely referring to a "soldier", for example.

Perhaps one of the most formidable problems lies in the lack of fixed surnames. A person was usually known by a given name and some variation of the place where the person resided. Before the standardization of spelling, names were written phonetically just as the ministers heard them. Thus Ten Eyck was written in the Moers register as von Eick, van Eijck, van Eick, ten Eicke, ten Eicken, ter Eick, von Eik, an gen Eick, an der Eick, an ger Eick, and an gen Eicken, all meaning "at or from the area of the oak." No evidence exists as to whether all or any of these persons were related. Even putting together the immediate family of Coenraet Ten Eyck tested the researcher's powers of deduction.

The first entry for Coenraet's father, Wilhelm an gen Eick (with spelling variations), is the baptism of an unnamed child:[7]

30 Apr. 1614, a child of Wilhelm an der Eick was baptized.

The next entry is a marriage:[8]

1 June 1614, Wilhelm an ger Eick and Michel Puitzen were married.

---

[5] G.S. No. 114,915, p. 160 (left).
[6] *Encyclopedia Britannica*, 15th ed., s.v. "Moers".
[7] G.S. No. 489,886, p. 42.
[8] Ibid., p. 45.

Of course the possibility exists that the first child was illegitimate. However, since the extant register does not begin until 1612 and no illegitimacy was mentioned, the even stronger assumption can be made that the child was by an earlier marriage before the beginning of records, and the child's baptism was delayed for some reason.

Additional evidence seems to support the theory of an earlier marriage. Three members of the Ten Eyck family witnessed the baptisms of Coenraet's children, and the given names of these witnesses were repeated frequently in subsequent generations, suggesting they may have been siblings. Since no additional information concerning these people was found in the Moers records which are available until 1636, and one would assume witnesses to be adults of at least 18 years, they would have been born no later than 1628. Therefore, the following tentative list is made of possible children by Wilhelm an gen Eick's first marriage:

    i.   Marija, b. ca. 1607.
   ii.   Jacob, b. ca. 1609.
  iii.   Andries, b. ca. 1611.
  iv.   Unnamed child, bap. 30 Apr. 1614.

The only children found for Wilhelm an gen Eick and Michel Puitzen could have been twins, or perhaps one was a delayed baptism, since they were baptized one day apart and over two years after the marriage:[9]

    i.   Conradt, bapt. 3 Mar. 1617.
   ii.   Anna, bap. 4 Mar. 1617; bur. 21 Jan. 1618.[10]

No burial record was found for either wife, but an additional marriage[11] was given:

15 Dec. 1628, Wilhelm an gen Eicken Funder and Greit Huten were married.

The word "Funder" became a curiosity. Was it a military rank, an occupation, a place, or an added surname? Since the Moers area was heavily fortified by soldiers, perhaps this was the military rank of "Fähnrich or Fehnrich, an officer, cadet, or ensign (Mil.)."[12]

Fortunately records for the Boel family were more complete, therefore, greater progress was made. As the marriage intention in Amsterdam stated, Coenraet Ten Eyck's wife, Maria Boel, was born in Cologne, Germany. Her parents, Tobias Boel and Margrieta van Apperloo, were not married there; however, their children were baptized in the Cologne Dutch Reformed Church:[13]

[9] Ibid., p. 78.
[10] Ibid., p. 89.
[11] Ibid., p. 245.
[12] *The New Cassell's German Dictionary*, rev. ed. (1965), s.v. "Fähnchen".
[13] G.S. No. 187,154, pp. 416, 418, 420, 422, 526, 527, 532, & 534.

i. Margarita, bap. 31 July 1606, wit: Franchoijs Boele and Janncken Tibautz.
ii. Heynderijch, bap. 1 June 1607, wit: Heyndrick Groudt; and Mareija Sonnemans, wife of Franss Franssens.
iii. Anna, bap. 11 Oct. 1608, wit: Heijndch Redthoffen, Luijtgen Pavasens, and Anna Appeloens.
iv. Janneken, bap. 13 July 1610, wit: Godhardus van Leen; and Josina Franssen, wife of Jan van Voonen.
v. Tobeijas, bap. 5 Feb. 1613, wit: Neijcolas Ruts and Janneken van Appelo.
vi. Conradt, bap. 10 Aug. 1614, wit: Conradt Sonnemanss and wife of Jorgen van der Sulss.
vii. Johannes, bap. 24 May 1619, wit: Johannes Creij and wife of Phillip der Curadt.
viii. Maria, bap. 15 July 1622, wit: Jeronijmus Maiquart; Marij Fromeau, wife of Nicolas Lintlau; and Marij Craij, daughter of Jacques Craij.

Many entries were found for other members of the Boel family in the registers of both the Dutch and French Reformed Churches of Cologne. Since only the direct line of Maria Boel,[14] wife of Conraet Ten Eyck, will be followed, these entries will not be given here. One exception is the marriage intention of Franchois Boel, the brother of Tobias Boel, which gives Antwerp, Belgium as his place of origin:

31 Mar. 1598, Franchois Boel, Jongman, filius Adriani, van Antwerp et Elisabeth Schuts, filia Diericks ooch van Antwerp de bruidegom var vergezelschapt met Jasper Sonnemans de bruid var vergezelschapt met Balthasar Schuts haar broeder welke van de bewillings haer moeder en de bruiden getuigen geeft.

Translation

31 Mar. 1598, Franchois Boel, young man, son of Adrian, from Antwerp; and Elizabeth Schuts, daughter of Dierick, also from Antwerp; the bridegroom was assisted by Jasper Sonnemans; the bride was assisted by Balthasar Schuts, her brother, who gave consent for the mother of the bride.

The question arises, what motivated almost the entire Boel family to migrate from Antwerp, Belgium to Cologne, Germany between 1589 and 1590? Soon after Luther posted his ninety-five propositions on the church door at Wittenberg on 31 October 1517, they became known throughout Belgium, especially in the large commercial center of Antwerp.

All those who read, bought, owned or spread Luther's works, including his translation of the New Testament, or attended so-called "heretic" meetings were punished by death. However, the Protestant movement continued to flourish.

At first the preaching was Lutheran. Then about 1540 Calvinism was also introduced into Belgium, and nearly the whole country was won over to the Reformation movement. In Antwerp alone, out of a population of 86,000, 50,000 became Calvinists.

Philip II, King of Spain, responded by sending his cruel Duke of Alva and Spanish troops into the Low Countries. The persecution that was then inflicted on Belgian Protestants was so intense, they were almost completely eliminated.

[14] Ibid. p. 603.

On 17 August 1585, Alessandro Farnese, Duke of Parma, conquered Antwerp. He gave the Calvinists four years to either revert to Catholicism or emigrate. Many made their way to Holland, England, and Germany, leaving Antwerp, once a prosperous harbour, desolate. Its warehouses stood empty; no ships docked there; and thousands of its houses were abandoned. Included among these refugees were members of the Boel family who chose Cologne, Germany as their new home.[15]

Although many Boel baptisms were found in the register of the Notre Dame Cathedral of Antwerp, only two were children of Adrian Boel and his wife Cornelia.[16] However, during this period of religious and civil unrest, it was not unusual for Protestants to have a few of their children baptized in the Catholic Church to give the impression they were devout Catholics, thereby escaping punishment or even death at the hands of their cruel oppressors. The baptism of an additional child, believed to be their last, was found in the Cologne Dutch Reformed Church.[17] The birth dates of other known children must be approximated:

    i.   Bartholomeus, b. ca. 1565, m. (1) bef. 1588, Catharina van Geel, in Antwerp; m. (2) 11 Nov. 1600, Anna de Coninck, in Cologne, Germany.
    ii. Frans, bap. 28 Sept. 1567, wit: Adrian de Laddrien, Jasper Sonnamens, Apolloni van Dael, and Leske Boels; m. 31 Mar. 1598, Elisabeth Schuts, Cologne, Germany.
    iii. Anna, bap. 7 Sept. 1568, wit: Franchoeys Vbalschaets, and Ana Capellen.
    iv. Catharina, b. ca. 1570, m. Denijs de Maistre.
    v.   Tobias, b. ca. 1572, m. Margarita van Apperloo.
    vi. Jacques, b. ca. 1574, m. Susanna van der Vindel.
    vii. Susanna, bap. 29 Oct. 1590, wit: Jan Flagelet; Catharina, wife of Denijs de Maistre; and Emmerentiana, wife of Cornelis Boot.

[15] H. van Duynen, "Protestantism in Belgium", *Proceedings of the Huguenot Society of London* 17 (1944): 234–236.
[16] G.S. No. 296,245, pp. 110 & 143 (left).
[17] G.S. No. 187,154, p. 268.

Appendix D

Magdalena Joire: A "Mademoiselle from Armentières," by Gwenn F. Epperson.

MAGDALENA JOIRE:
A "MADEMOISELLE FROM ARMENTIERES" [1]

BY GWENN F. EPPERSON*

Much is known concerning the French background of Matthew Blanchan, farmer from Artois, who came to New Netherland in *De Vergulde Otter* (The Gilded Otter) on 26 April 1660 with a wife and three children (HSYB 1902:16). His early life in France is well documented in a small pamphlet, *Matthew Blanchan in Europe and America*, from the papers of Major Louis DuBois (1891–1965), revised and enlarged by Ruth P. Heidgerd (New Paltz, New York: DuBois Family Association, Huguenot Historical Society, 1979). However, reference to his wife Magdalena Joire is confined to one paragraph on the first page:

> Some time before 1635, he [Matthew Blanchan] moved to Armentières, very near the Belgian border, and married Magdeleine Jorisse or Joire. The recent translation of the Mannheim records [French Congregation at Mannheim] make us wonder if this was a patronymic. In one place her name is given as "Madeleine Serge" and we wonder if her father's name could be Joris Serge. Did his family, perhaps, have something to do with the development of that twilled fabric so important to the textile industry around Lille? This is sheer speculation.

Although the name of Matthew Blanchan's wife is consistently given in documents as "Magdalena Joire," including its several variations, once she is listed as "Madelaine Serge," as referenced above. On 15 July 1654 in the Registers of the French Congregation at Mannheim, 1651–1710, "Madelaine Serge, wife of Mathieu Blanchon" appears as one of the godmothers at the baptism of Marguerite, daughter of Hugue Malbrancq and Marguerite Desobrye (extract from the register, courtesy of Ruth P. Heidgerd).

The premise, that "Joire" was the father's given name and "Serge" the surname, appears logical. However, a study of the Roman Catholic Church Registers of Armentières, Département du Nord, France (formerly French Flanders) does not prove it correct. In fact Magdalena Joire was the daughter of Petrus** Joire and Jacoba Le Blan or Le Blanc, and was baptized 27 October 1611, godparents Bartholomeus Le Blanc and Magdelena Gruson (Baptisms Roman Catholic Church of Armentières, France, 1590–1621, transcribed and indexed, #3001, FHL 1,122,756).

Petrus Joire was born *circa* 1575, his wife Jacoba Le Blanc was born *circa* 1579, and they were married *circa* 1600, all dates estimated from the birth of their first child in 1601. Armentières baptisms do not begin until 1590 and marriages until 1632, therefore, nothing further was found there concerning Magdelena's parents.

The surname "Serge" is not found in the index to baptisms of the Roman Catholic Church of Armentières, 1590–1621 (FHL 1,122,756), whereas the sur-

[1](From *The New York Genealogical and Biographical Record*, Vol. 122, Number 2, April 1991.)

* 3349 South 350 West, Bountiful, Utah 84010.
** Most of the first names used in this article are Latin forms found in the church registers. "Petrus" (usually recorded in the genitive, "Petri") was probably "Pierre" in everyday life. (Ed.)

name "Joire" is quite prevalent, as also "Le Blan" or "Le Blanc." According to
the *Dictionnaire Etymologique des Noms de Famille et Prénoms de France*, the etymo-
logical study of surnames and given names of France by Albert Dauzat, reviewed
and enlarged by Marie Thérèse Morlet (Paris: Librairie Larousse, 1970), page
345, the name "Joire" is an archaic form of "George." Therefore, it is entirely
possible it was a patronymic at one time. However, it is evident "Joire" was an
established surname by the time the Armentières registers began in 1590.

Dauzat's dictionary also includes the name "Blanc" or "Blanche" (page 46)
which are the masculine and feminine forms of the adjective "white or fair."
Its many variations include even "Blanchon" which is probably the origin of
Matthew Blanchan's surname.

Although Petrus Joire had six children baptized in the Roman Catholic
Church, very few other Joires had more than one or two baptized there, leading
to the belief they were Huguenots. There were a large number of Huguenots
in the towns on the present border between France and Belgium, or the area
of Flanders, i.e., Tourcoing, Valenciennes, St. Amand, Armentières, Tournai,
Lille and Cambrai. These towns were the chief centers of emigration from the
Spanish Inquisition which then had authority in the area.

Since Flanders is no longer a political entity, perhaps an explanation is in
order. According to the *Encyclopedia Britannica* (15th ed., Vol. 4, p. 817):

> Flanders, French *Flandre*, Flemish *Vlaanderen*, medieval principality in the southwest of the
> Low Countries which included what are now the French "department" of Nord, the Belgian
> provinces of East Flanders and West Flanders, and the Dutch province of Zeeland. The
> name appeared as early as the 8th century and is believed to mean Lowland.
> . . . Through the marriage of Charles [the Bold's] daughter Mary to Maximilian of Aus-
> tria, Flanders fell to and remained under Spanish (and later Austrian) Hapsburg rule from
> the 15th to the 17th centuries, suffering severe territorial losses to France under Louis XIV.
> It disappeared as a political entity in the course of the French Revolutionary wars.

For those readers who may have difficulty relating to the present article's sub-
title, A "Mademoiselle from Armentières," the *Encyclopedia* says (Vol. 1, p. 568):

> Armentières, town, Nord "department," Nord-Pas-de-Calais region, northern France, on
> the Lys River, near the Belgian frontier . . . Armentières was 2 mi. (3 km.) behind the
> battle line throughout World War I, and from April until September 1918, it was occupied
> by the Germans. The marching song about the mythical "Mademoiselle from Armentières"
> sung by British and U.S. troops dates from that period.

Petrus Joire had six children baptized in the Roman Catholic Church of Armentières, but his wife Jacoba Le Blan is only mentioned in the first child's
baptismal record. Shortly thereafter the priest eliminates the mothers' names
completely. However, it is known Jacoba was alive until at least 26 August 1608
when she appears as a godmother at the baptism of Daniel Le Blan son of
Joannis, in the same parish register as referenced above (FHL 1,122,756 #1912).
There is a gap of eight years between the last two Joire children, suggesting
the possible death of Jacoba and a remarriage.

Children of Petrus Joire and Jacoba Le Blanc, baptized in the Roman Catholic Church of Armentières (FHL 1,122,756):

i. Maria, bap. 1 Oct. 1601, godparents: Tobias Le Blan; Maria Gillon, Gudon[us] Joire's wife (#2808).

ii. Margareta, bap. 24 Jan. 1604, godparents: Philippus Grenie, Margarita Le Blan (#296).

iii. Joannes, bap. 8 Feb. 1605, godparents: Joannes Le Blan, Maria Breton (#654).

iv. Joanna, bap. 14 Aug. 1608, godparents: Carolus Joire, Joanna Brison (#1899).

v. Magdalena, bap., 27 Oct. 1611, godparents: Bartholomeus Le Blanc, Magdalena Gruson (#3001).

vi. Petrus, bap. 4 Oct. 1619, godparents: Michael Berton, Maria Becgeu (#2749).

Since beginning this article the marriage of Matthew Blanchan and Magdalena Joire was found in the registers of the same church as above (Marriages Roman Catholic Church of Armentières, 1630–1736, FHL 1,122,754). As this information has not been published to date, according to the author's knowledge, it is included here:

15 Oct. 1633 Cont. Mat., Mattheus blanchart et Mag la Joire test. Petrus Joire et Michaele de lestre.

[Translation] 15 Oct. 1633 Contracted Marriage, Mattheus Blanchart and Magdalena Joire, witnesses Petrus Joire and Michaele de Lestre.

Another interesting find was the baptismal record of an additional child of this couple in the same church (Baptisms Roman Catholic Church of Armentières, 1640–1648, FHL 1,133,313), which reads:

14 August. 1642, baptizatus fuit Maximilianus Blanchart filius Mathei et Magdalenae Joire. Pubr. Maximilanus Lalau, et Joanna Cousmart.

[Translation] 14 August 1642, was baptized Maximilianus Blanchart son of Matheus and Magdalena Joire. Godparents Maximilanus Lalau, and Joanna Cousmart.

BIBLIOGRAPHY

The following list is not intended to include all sources available for New Netherland research. It is a compilation of those which the author has found useful. The journal articles on the origins of specific families are only a few of the hundreds of articles that have been published.

Bailey, Rosalie Fellows. "Dutch Systems in Family Naming: New York and New Jersey." *National Genealogical Society Quarterly* 47 (1953): 1-11; 109-18. Reprinted as National Genealogical Society Special Publication No. 12, 1965.

------------. "Emigrants to New Netherland: Account Book 1654-1664." *New York Genealogical and Biographical Record* 94 (1963): 193-200.

Bentz, Edna M. *If I Can, You Can Decipher Germanic Records.* San Diego: E. M. Bentz, 1982.

Bottin des communes. Paris: Didot-Bottin, 1988.

Boyer, Carl, 3rd. *Ship Passenger Lists: New York and New Jersey (1600-1825)* Newhall, Calif.: the compiler, 1978.

Brouwer, Hans. *Beknopte handleiding tot de kennis van het Nederlandsche oude schrift.* Naarden: N.V. Uitgevers and Maatschappi A. Rutgers, 1941.

------------. *Geschreven Verleden: genealogie en oud schrift.* s'Gravenhage: Europese Bibliotheek. 1963.

Calendar of New Jersey Wills. 1670-1817. Archives of the State of New Jersey. First Series, vols. 23, 30, 32-42. Trenton, N.J.: 1901-1949. *Cassell's New Latin Dictionary: Latin-English, English-Latin.* New York: Funk & Wagnalls, 1968.

Centrum voor Familiegeschiedenis. *Oud schrift: kursus per briefwisseling.* 3 vols. Antwerp; n.p., 1968.

Cerny, Johni and Wendy Elliott. *The Library.* Salt Lake City: Ancestry Publishing Co., 1988.

Chadwick, Owen, ed. *The Reformation. The Pelican History of the Church,* vol. 3. Harmondsworth, Eng.: Penguin Books, 1964. Reprint, 1975.

Christiansen, Henry E. *Searching for Scandinavian Ancestors at the Genealogical Society Library.* Salt Lake City: Genealogical Society of The Church of Jesus Christ of Latter-day Saints, 1969.

Cross, Francis William. *History of the Walloon and Huguenot Church at Canterbury.* Publications of the Huguenot Society of London, vol. 15. Canterbury: Cross & Jackman, 1898.

Dauzat, Albert. *Dictionnaire Étymologique des Noms de Famille et Prénoms de France.* Reviewed and enlarged by Marie Thérèse Morlet. Paris: Larousse, 1980.

Der Grosse Conti Auto-Atlas. Munich: JRO Kartografische Verlagsgesellschaft, 1983.

Dern, John Philip, ed. *The Albany Protocol.* Ann Arbor, Michigan: Dern, 1971.

De Seyn, Eugene. *Geschieden aardrijkskundig woordenboek der Belgische gemeente.* 2 vols. Turnhout: Brepols, 1941-.

Douxchamps, Hervé and Reymond Tefnin. *Repertorium der oude parochieregisters in België*. Brussels: Hervé Douxchamps, 1985.

Dubois, Major Louis. *Matthew Blanchan in Europe and America*. Revised and enlarged by Ruth P. Heidgard. New Paltz, New York: Dubois Family Association, Huguenot Historical Society, 1979.

Encyclopaedia Britannica, 1986 ed. s.v. "Belgium."

Epperson, Gwenn F. "Another Low Family of New York and New Jersey." *New York Genealogical and Biographical Record* 119 (1988): 193-201; 120 (1989): 35-43, 104-07.

------------. "The European Ancestry of Egbert van Borsum and Annetje Hendricks." *New York Genealogical and Biographical Record* 119 (1988): 84-89.

------------. "The European Origin of the Hardenbrook Family." *New York Genealogical and Biographical Record* 117 (1986): 1-7.

------------. "Jacob Hellekers Alias Swart and Some of His Descendants." *New York Genealogical and Biographical Record* 121 (1990): 13-18, 76-83, 164-68, 216-20.

------------. "Jan Evertsen, Master Shoemaker of Albany." *New York Genealogical and Biographical Record*, in press.

------------. "Magdalena Joire: A Mademoiselle from Armentières." *New York Genealogical and Biographical Record* 122 (1991): 85-87.

------------. "The Ten Eyck-Boel European Connection." *New York Genealogical and Biographical Record* 118 (1987): 13-18.

Evjen, John Oluf. *Scandinavian Immigrants in New York, 1630-1674*. Minneapolis: K.C. Holter Publishing Co. 1916. Reprint. Baltimore: Genealogical Publishing Co., 1972.

Fernow, Berthold, trans. and ed. *The Minutes of the Orphanmasters of New Amsterdam, 1655-1663*. 2 vols. New York: Francis P. Harper, 1902-07.

------------, trans. *The Records of New Amsterdam from 1653-1674*, 7 vols. 1897. Reprint. Baltimore: Genealogical Publishing Co., 1976.

Fisher, George B. *The Reformation*. New York: Charles Scribner's Sons, 1886.

Gehring, Charles T., trans. and ed. *Fort Orange Court Minutes, 1652-1660*. Syracuse: Syracuse University Press, 1990.

------------, trans. and ed. *New York Historical Manuscripts: Dutch*. vol. 5, *Council Minutes, 1652-1654*. Baltimore: Genealogical Publishing Co., 1983.

Gemeentelijke Archiefdienst Amsterdam. *Inhoudsopgaaf . . . te Amsterdam over de jaren 1875-1897*. Amsterdam: Het Archief, n.d.

Geyl, Pieter. *The Netherlands in the Seventeenth Century*. 2 vols. London: Ernest Benn, 1961.

Grimm, Harold John. *The Reformation Era, 1500-1650*. New York: Macmillan Co., 1973.

Haberkern, Eugen and Joseph Friedrich Wallach. *Hilfswör terbuch für Historiker: Mittelalter und Neuzeit*. Bern and Munich: Francke Verlag, 1964.

Hoes, Roswell Randall, ed. *Baptismal and Marriage Registers of the Old Dutch Church of Kingston, Ulster County, New York, 1660-1809*. Baltimore: Genealogical Publishing Co., 1980.

Hoffman, William J. "Random Notes Concerning Settlers of Dutch Descent." *The American Genealogist* 29 (1953): 65-76, 146-52; 30 (1954): 138-44.

Hovenden, Robert, ed. *The Registers of the Walloon or Strangers' Church in Canterbury*. Publications of the Huguenot Society of London, vol. 5, pts. 1-3. Lymington, Eng.: C.T. King, 1891-98.

The Huguenot Historian. The Huguenot Society of New Jersey, 1980-82.

Huizinga, A. *Encyclopedie van voornamen*. Amsterdam: A. J. G. Strengholt's, 1957.

Johansson, Carl-Erik. *Cradled in Sweden: A Practical Help to Genealogical Research in Swedish Records*. Logan, Utah: Everton Publishers, 1972.

Kiessling, Hermann, comp. *Trauungen Kirchspielfremder in Elberfeld (Reformed), 1585-1620 und 1649-1675*. Wuppertal-Wohwinkel: Verlag Bergisch Land der Westdeutschen Gesellschaft für Familienkunde, 1970.

Konigliche Preussische Landesaufnahme. Scale 1:100, 000 Berlin: Die Landesaufnahme, 1914-17.

Kuyper, J. *Gemeente-Atlas van Nederland: naar officieele bronnen bewerkt*. 11 vols. Leeuwarden: Hugo Suringar, 1955.

"List of Emigrants to New Netherland, 1654-1664." Ms. pamphlet in Box 23, James Riker Collection, Rare Books and Manuscripts Division, New York Public Library.

Macy, Harry, Jr. "Bradt Records from Amsterdam." *New York Genealogical and Biographical Record* 118 (1987): 133-34.

------------. "Jochem Kaller/Caljer/Colyer: His Place of Origin Identified." *New York Genealogical and Biographical Record* 121 (1990): 36.

------------. "New Light on the Origin of Joost Duryea." *New York Genealogical and Biographical Record* 121 (1990): 34-35.

Meijers, J. A. and J. C. Luitingh. *Onze voornamen*. Amsterdam: Moussault's Uitgeverij, 1966.

Moens, William John Charles. *The Walloons and Their Church at Norwich: Their History and Registers, 1565-1832.* Publications of the Huguenot Society of London, vol. 1. Lymington, Eng.: R. E. King & C. King, 1887-88.

Motley, John Lothrop. *History of the United Netherlands* . . . 4 vols. New York: Harper & Bros., 1870.

New York Colonial Manuscripts, vol. 14, formerly book KK, Accounts 1654-1664, original in New York State Archives.

O'Callaghan, Edmund Bailey. *History of New Netherland.* 2 vols. New York: D'Appleton & Co., 1846-48.

------------. ed. *The Documentary History of the State of New York*, (4 vols. in 8). Albany: Weed, Parson & Co., public printers 1849.

------------. ed. *Lists of Inhabitants of Colonial New York.* Baltimore: Genealogical Publishing Co., 1979.

------------. trans. "Dutch Records in the City Clerk's Office, New York." Extracts from Dutch documents bound in a book labeled "Original Records of Burgomasters and Orphan Masters." *Year Book of the Holland Society of New York* 1900: 110-12.

------------. trans., "Walewyn Van der Veen's Records, 1662-1664." *Year Book of the Holland Society of New York 1900*: 152-58; FHL 0908989, it. 4.

------------. trans., *The Minutes of the Orphanmasters of New Amsterdam, 1663-1668*. ed. Kenn Stryker-Rodda and Kenneth Scott. Baltimore: Genealogical Publishing Co., 1976.

------------. trans., *New York Historical Manuscripts: Dutch, The Register of Salomon Lachaire, Notary Public of New Amsterdam, 1661-1662*, ed. Kenneth Scott and Kenn Stryker-Rodda. Baltimore: Genealogical Publishing Co., 1978.

------------. comp. "Settlers in Rensselaerswyck from 1630 to 1646." *Year Book of the Holland Society of New York* 1896: 130-40.

O'Callaghan, Edmund Bailey and Berthold Fernow, trans. and eds. *Documents Relative to the Colonial History of the State of New York*. 15 vols. Albany: Weed, Parson & Co., 1856-87.

Oud schrift: kursus per briefwisseling. 3 vols. Antwerp: Centrum voor Familiegeschiedenis, 1968.

Praetorius, Otfried. *Kirchenbücher und Standesregister für alle Wohnplätze im Land Hessen*. Darmstadt: Selbstverlag der Historischen Kommission für das Land Hessen, 1939.

Purple, Samuel S., ed. *Marriages from 1639 to 1801 in the Reformed Dutch Church of New Amsterdam and New York City*. Collections of the New York Genealogical and Biographical Society, vol. 1. Reprint.vol. 9. 1940.

Roodenberg, C. "Genealogical Research Problems in the Netherlands." Lecture given at the *World Conference on Records and Genealogical Seminar*, sponsored by The Church of Jesus Christ of Latter-day Saints, Salt Lake City, Utah, 5-8 August 1969. Published in pamphlet Area D5 & 6e.

Slok, Hendrik O. "The Dutch Ancestry of the Van Barkello Family in Early Kings County New York: in the Netherlands." *New York Genealogical and Biographical Record* 115 (1984): 193-98.

------------. "The Provost Family in the Netherlands." *New York Genealogical and Biographical Record* 113 (1932): 1-9.

Smiles, Samuel. *The Huguenots, Their Settlements, Churches, and Industries in England and Ireland*. 6th. ed. London: John Murray, 1889.

Smit, Pamela and J. W. Smit, comps. and eds. *The Netherlands: A Chronology and Fact Book, 57 B.C.-1971*. Dobbs Ferry, N.Y.: Oceana Publishers, 1973.

Smith, Frank and Finn A. Thomsen. *Genealogical Guidebook and Atlas of Norway*. Logan, Utah: Everton Publishers, 1974.

Smith, Frank and Finn A. Thomsen, comps. *Genealogical Guidebook and Atlas of Denmark*. Bountiful, Utah: Thomsen's Genealogical Center, 1986.

Stryker-Rodda, Kenn. "New Netherland Naming Systems and Customs." Lecture given at the *World Conference on Records and Genealogical Seminar.* Sponsored by the Church of Jesus Christ of Latter-day Saints, Salt Lake City, Utah, 5-8 August 1969. Published in pamphlet Area 1-27.

Sturm, Heribert. *Unsere Schrift.* Neustadt on the Aisch and Munich: Degner Verlag, 1961.

Uetrecht, E., comp. *Meyers Orts- und Verkehrs-lexikon des Deutschen Reichs.* 2 vols. Leipzig: Bibliographisches Institut, 1912-13.

Van Cleef, Frank L., trans. "Baptisms, Marriages and Other Records from the Reformed Protestant Dutch Church of Flatbush, Kings County, New York." Copied by Josephine C. Frost. Manuscript in possession of the New York Genealogical and Biographical Society.

Van der Aa, Abraham Jacobus, comp. *Aardrijkskundig woordenboek der Nederlanden.* 14 vols. Gorinchem: Jacobus Noorduyn en Zoon, 1839-51. Reprint 1979.

Van der Linde, A. P. G. Jos, trans. and ed. *New York Historical Manuscripts: Dutch, Old First Dutch Reformed Church of Brooklyn, New York: First Book of Records, 1660-1752.* Baltimore: Genealogical Publishing Co., 1983.

Van der Plank, A. N. W. *Het namenboek.* Bussum: Unieboek bv., 1979.

Van der Schaar. *Woordenboek van voornamen.* 5th ed. Utrecht: Uitgerverij het Spectrum, 1970.

Van Duynen, H. "Protestantism in Belgium." *Proceedings of the Huguenot Society of London.* 18 vols. and supp. n.d. 17:231.

Van Gelder, A. Margaretha. *Amsterdamsche straatnamen: geschiedkundig verklaard*. Amsterdam: P. N. van Kampen & Zoon, 1913.

Van Gent, L. F. *Een wereldreis van 2000 huismarken met 2170 teekeningen*. Arnhem: S. Gouda Quint-D. Brouwer en Zoon, 1944.

Van Goor, G. B. *Dutch-English, English-Dutch Van Goor Dictionary*. s'Gravenhage: G. B. Van Goor, 1938.

Van Laer, Arnold Johan Ferdinand, trans. and ed. *Minutes of the Court of Albany, Rensselaerswyck, and Schenectady, 1668-1685*. 3 vols. Albany: University of New York, 1926-32.

------------, trans. and ed. *Minutes of the Court of Rensselaerswyck, 1648-1652*. Albany: University of the State of New York, 1922.

------------, trans. *New York Historical Manuscripts: Dutch*. Vol. 4. *Council Minutes, 1638-1649*, ed. Kenneth Scott and Kenn Stryker-Rodda. Baltimore: Genealogical Publishing Co., 1974.

------------, trans. *New York Historical Manuscripts: Dutch, Registers of the Provincial Secretary, 1638-1660*. 3 vols. ed. Kenneth Scott and Kenn Stryker-Rodda. Baltimore: Genealogical Publishing Co., 1974.

------------, trans. "Passengers to New Netherland, 1654-1664." *Year Book of the Holland Society of New York* 1902: 1-37.

------------, trans. and ed. *Van Rensselaer Bowier Manuscripts*. Albany: University of the State of New York, 1908.

------------, ed. *Notarial Papers 1 and 2, 1660-1696*. Vol. 3 of Jonathan Pearson, trans. *Early Records of the City and County of Albany and Colony of Rensselaerswyck*, 4 vols. Albany: University of the State of New York, 1869-1919.

Van Resandt, W. Wijnaendts. *Repertorium DTB*. ed. and comp. J. G. J. van Booma. 2nd print. s'Gravenhage: Centraal bureau voor genealogie, 1980.

Versteeg, Dingman, trans. *New York Historical Manuscripts: Dutch, Kingston Papers, 1661-1675*. 2 vols. ed. Peter R. Christoph, Kenneth Scott, and Kenn Stryker-Rodda. Baltimore: Genealogical Publishing Co., 1976.

Versteeg, Dingman and Thomas E. Vermilye, Jr., trans. and eds. *Bergen Records, Records of the Reformed Protestant Dutch Church of Bergen in New Jersey, 1666 to 1788*. 3 bks. in 1. Baltimore: Genealogical Publishing Co., 1976.

www.ingramcontent.com/pod-product-compliance
Lightning Source LLC
Chambersburg PA
CBHW061742270326
41928CB00011B/2342

* 9 7 8 0 8 0 6 3 1 4 0 0 6 *